# COOKS IN PARKS

A COLLECTION OF RECIPES BY THOSE WHO LOVE, ENJOY AND SUPPORT OUR
NATIONAL AND STATE PARKS IN SOUTH DAKOTA, WYOMING AND BEYOND

Published by Badlands Natural History Association, Black Hills Parks & Forests Association,
Devils Tower Natural History Association and the Mount Rushmore Bookstores
Reviewed by Mount Rushmore National Memorial Chief of Interpretation Maureen McGee-Ballinger and
Devils Tower National Monument Chief of Interpretation Nancy Stimson
Edited by Debbie M. Ketel
Copy Editor: Mary Anne Maier
Designed by Ponderosa Pine Design, Vicky Vaughn Shea
Project Manager: Debbie M. Ketel
Printed in the U.S.A., using vegetable-based inks on FSC®-certified paper, containing 10% PCW

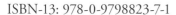

ISBN-13: 978-0-9798823-7-1
More information on the parks included within may be found at:
www.badlandsnha.org
www.devilstowernha.org
www.blackhillsparks.org
www.mountrushmoresociety.com
www.nps.gov

# COOKS IN PARKS

A COLLECTION OF RECIPES BY THOSE WHO LOVE, ENJOY AND SUPPORT OUR NATIONAL AND STATE PARKS IN SOUTH DAKOTA, WYOMING AND BEYOND

A Stories in Stone Publication
Badlands Natural History Association, Black Hills Parks & Forests Association
Devils Tower Natural History Association, Mount Rushmore Bookstores

# CONTENTS

CUSTER STATE PARK IS A
PLACE WHERE ONE CAN STILL
BE AN UNWORRIED AND
UNREGIMENTED INDIVIDUAL
AND WEAR ANY OLD CLOTHES
AND SIT ON A LOG AND GET
HIS SANITY BACK AGAIN

# INTRODUCTION

This book is a collection of recipes by those who love, enjoy and support our national and state parks in South Dakota, Wyoming and beyond. National parks and state parks were set aside for the preservation and enjoyment of the American people. We are inspired and rejuvenated by the beauty and the stories they speak. In order to maintain these treasures, the national and state parks in the Black Hills region have relied on nonprofit organizations such as Badlands Natural History Association, Black Hills Parks & Forests Association, Devils Tower Natural History Association and the Mount Rushmore Bookstores to raise funds in a variety of ways to supplement federal and state budgets.

In partnering together, these organizations have created this publication as a legacy to the food and parks we enjoy. A portion of proceeds from the sale of this book goes back to the national and/or state parks they support so that park supporters (like you!) can enjoy them for years to come.

# *Breakfast*

## WIND CAVE NATIONAL PARK

Swaying prairie grasses, forested hillsides and an array of wildlife (such as bison, elk and prairie dog) welcome visitors to Wind Cave National Park, one of our country's oldest national parks and one of its few remaining intact prairies. Wind Cave is one of the world's longest caves. Named for barometric winds at its entrance, this complex labyrinth of passages contains boxwork, an unusual calcite cave formation resembling honeycomb.

LOCATED NEAR HOT SPRINGS, SD
Supported by Black Hills Parks & Forests Association

*"Have given up the idea of finding the end of Wind Cave."*
*—Alvin McDonald, January 23, 1891*

**Bison call Wind Cave National Park home.**

# Trappers Breakfast

My nephews and son make Trappers Breakfast when they camp. It's great and can be adjusted to a baked dish at home. It is simply this . . .

Eggs scrambled, any amount

Broccoli

Bacon

Onions

Salt, pepper and cook in container over the campfire.

KAY JORGENSEN
Mount Rushmore Society

# Overnight Caramel French Toast

- 1 cup brown sugar
- 1 tsp cinnamon
- ½ cup butter or margarine
- 6 eggs
- 2 T corn syrup
- 1½ cups milk
- 12 slices bread
- 1 tsp vanilla
- ¼ cup sugar

In a saucepan over medium heat, bring to a boil brown sugar, butter or margarine and corn syrup, stirring constantly. Pour into a 9 x 13-inch pan.

Top with 6 slices of bread. Combine sugar and cinnamon. Sprinkle ½ of this mixture over bread. Top with remaining 6 slices of bread.

Sprinkle with remaining cinnamon/sugar mixture. Mix together remaining ingredients and pour over all. Cover and chill overnight. Remove.

Bake uncovered at 350° for 30–35 minutes.

KAREN MEYER
Black Hills Parks & Forests Association

# Hearty Jorgensen Pancakes

My grandmothers, my mom and I have all used breakfast for a special purpose. They used these hearty, thin pancakes to prepare us for chores and long days.

I used the meal to keep my kids and their friends close. Summer Sundays found pancakes the center of a whole neighborhood gathering. I can't tell you the hours of fun and conversation and memories that exist because I could fry, serve and listen. The benefit to the cook is that these pancakes are best served hot, so eating is not for the cook. I know it is why my mom was so tiny!

| | |
|---|---|
| 1 | cup flour |
| 2 | eggs |
| 1 | tsp salt |
| ⅛ | tsp baking powder |
| 3+ | cups half & half, use all necessary to make batter very thin |

Mix all together but don't over-mix. Obviously this can be doubled for more servings.

Use an iron skillet with oil. I like to use saved bacon grease. The skillet needs to be very hot as the pancake cooks quickly. Just pour a small amount into the pan, swirl to spread, flip once and serve.

We love syrup, butter and sugar or chokecherry syrup for toppings.

*"Our parks provide comfort in time of stress, sunshine for our joy and strength when we doubt. They always stand as an example of the best in us all. When my children were little, we often traveled to visit the presidents. They, 'The Presidents,' always answered the call, and do today, for those little ones (now grown) who so long ago played at the foot of the mountain."*

KAY JORGENSEN
Mount Rushmore Society

# Biscuit and Gravy Bites

1 lb spicy pork sausage

1 pkg (8 oz) cream cheese, softened

1 pkg refrigerator Crescent sheets. If unavailable, use rolls and pinch together at perforations.

Preheat oven to 375°. Spray 8 x 8-inch pan with non-stick spray.

Brown sausage and drain well. Add cream cheese. Heat and stir until smooth.

Spread ½ of the Crescent sheet onto the bottom of pan.

Add sausage/cheese mixture and spread evenly over Crescent sheet layer.

Top with remaining ½ of Crescent sheet, spreading to edges.

Bake 20 minutes or until top is golden brown. Cut into squares.

*"I love national parks because they are OURS. They belong to all of us. They are located on the best and most unique tracts of land in our country and kept out of the reach of private landowners and developers so we can all enjoy them."*

DAWN MILLER
Garretson, SD

# *Bread*

## JEWEL CAVE NATIONAL MONUMENT

With over 168 miles of mapped and surveyed passages, Jewel Cave is one of the longest caves in the world. Its splendor is revealed through fragile formations and glimpses of brilliant color. Its maze of passages lures explorers, and its scientific wealth remains a mystery.

LOCATED NEAR CUSTER, SD
Supported by Black Hills Parks & Forests Association

*"The excitement of discovery,*
*The elation and despair,*
*The thrill of pushing forward to*
*Discover what is there."*
*—Jan Conn,* Jewel Cave Adventure

**The Townsend's big-eared bat makes its home at Jewel Cave National Monument.**

# Believe-It-or-Not Banana Bread

¼ cup butter

¾ cup sugar

2 eggs

2 cups Bisquick or other pancake mix

3 medium mashed bananas

½ tsp vanilla

Mix all together and bake in a loaf pan at 350˚ for about 55 minutes. Raisins, pecans, walnuts or other nuts can be added to the mixture as well.

KAREN POPPE
Wall, SD

# Farmhouse Barbecue Muffins

1 tube (10 oz) refrigerated buttermilk biscuits

1 lb ground beef, browned and drained

½ cup ketchup

3 T brown sugar

1 T cider vinegar

½ tsp chili powder

1 cup (4 oz) shredded cheddar cheese

Separate dough into 10 biscuits.

Flatten into 5-inch circles.

Press each into the bottom and up the sides of a greased muffin cup. Set aside.

In a small bowl, mix ketchup, brown sugar, vinegar and chili powder. Stir until smooth.

Add to meat and mix well.

Divide the meat mixture among biscuit-lined muffin cups, using about ¼ cup for each.

Sprinkle with cheese.

Bake at 375° for 18-20 minutes or until golden brown.

Cool for 5 minutes before removing from tin and serving.

Yield: 10 servings.

AMY KLEIN-GREBA
Devils Tower, WY

# Jalapeño Corn Muffins

MIX

| | | | |
|---|---|---|---|
| 1 | cup flour | 1 | T baking powder |
| 1 | cup yellow cornmeal | 1 | tsp red pepper flakes |
| ¼ | cup sugar | | |

WHISK

| | | | |
|---|---|---|---|
| 1 | egg | ¼ | cup vegetable oil |
| ½ | cup + 1 T milk | 1 | can (17 oz) creamed corn |

Stir all of the above lightly (15-20 strokes). Fill paper-lined muffin tins about ½ full. Reserve about ⅓ of the batter. Make a small depression in the muffin and drop in about ⅓ tsp jalapeño jelly. Divide reserved batter to cover jelly. Bake at 375° for 25 minutes or until light golden brown. Let muffins rest in pan for 2 minutes before removing. Cool on wire rack.

Yield: 1 dozen

RUTH SAMUELSEN
Mount Rushmore Society

## RUTH'S JALAPEÑO JELLY

This recipe came from a friend of my son's great-grandmother from Hettinger, ND. Hettinger is not far from Theodore Roosevelt National Park, which we have enjoyed visiting.

| | | | |
|---|---|---|---|
| ½ | cup grated jalapeños, seeded | 6½ | cups sugar |
| ¾ | cup green pepper, grated | 1½ | cups brown (cider) vinegar |

Mix and leave overnight.

Bring to boil, without straining out the pulp.

Add 1 package liquid Certo. Use both packets.

2 drops food coloring (optional).

Boil exactly 1 minute. Skim off foam.

Yield: 6 cups.

# Zucchini Fritters

For those who, like me, end up with an overabundance of zucchini from their garden (or their friends' gardens), this is a great recipe in which to use it.

| | | | |
|---|---|---|---|
| 2 | medium zucchinis | 1 | tsp kosher salt |
| ¼ | cup grated onion | ½ | tsp black pepper |
| 2 | eggs, lightly beaten | 1 | T butter |
| 6 | T flour | 1 | T olive oil |

Grate zucchini and onion into bowl and squeeze out any excess liquid.

Add eggs, salt, pepper and flour.

Heat a large skillet over medium heat and melt butter and oil together in the pan. When warm, drop heaping spoons of batter into pan and lightly flatten with spatula.

Cook fritters approximately 2-3 minutes on each side until browned.

Lightly sprinkle finished fritters with kosher salt and serve immediately.

Wipe out skillet with dry paper towel and add more butter and oil to pan before frying more fritters. Fritters can be kept warm in 300° oven.

*"Each park is a treasured resource and belongs to everyone."*

DEBI WHITE, NORTH DISTRICT MANAGER
Redwood Parks Association

# Cranberry Orange Scones

2 cups all-purpose flour

10 tsp sugar, divided

1 T grated orange peel

2 tsp baking powder

½ tsp salt

¼ tsp baking soda

⅓ cup cold butter

1 cup dried cranberries (or any dried berry)

¼ cup orange juice

¼ cup half & half

1 egg

1 T milk

Preheat oven to 400˚.

Combine flour, 2 tsp sugar, orange peel, baking powder, salt and baking soda.

Cut in butter until mixture is course crumbs. Set aside.

In small bowl, combine berries, orange juice, cream and egg.

Add to flour mixture and stir until soft dough forms.

On floured surface, gently knead 8-10 times. Pat into an 8-inch circle.

Cut into 10 wedges.

Separate wedges and place on ungreased cookie sheet.

Brush with milk and sprinkle with remaining sugar.

Bake for 12-15 minutes or until lightly browned.

GLAZE

½ cup confectioners' sugar

1 T orange juice

Combine and drizzle over scones.

DAWN MILLER
Garretson, SD

# Baking Powder Biscuits

Here's a recipe from my mom, Linda Lintz, who lives on a ranch next to Gutzon Borglum's ranch in Hermosa, SD. She grew up with the sculptor's grandchildren, Robin Borglum and Jim Borglum. These biscuits only take 20 minutes to make from start to finish and will melt in your mouth!

¾ cup milk or cream

## IN A MIXING BOWL, COMBINE

½ cup butter, softened

2 cups flour

1 tsp salt

3 tsps baking powder

With a fork, sift and mix the butter and dry ingredients together until crumbly.

Add milk and mix just enough to form loose dough. Do not knead or over-mix!

Gently roll dough onto floured surface and use a cookie cutter or water glass to cut 3-inch biscuits.

Place side by side on ungreased cookie sheet or cake pan.

Bake at 450° for 12 minutes. Enjoy hot with butter and jam or honey.

MARNIE HERRMANN
Mount Rushmore Society

# Cinnamon Crumb Cake

### BATTER

- 1 pkg yellow cake mix
- 1 pkg (small) vanilla instant pudding
- 3 T oil
- 1 ⅓ cups water
- 2 eggs

Preheat oven to 350°.

In large bowl, mix batter ingredients. Beat 2 minutes at medium speed. Do not over-mix!

### CRUMBS

- 1 cup of flour
- 1 cup sugar
- 3 tsp cinnamon
- 2 T melted margarine (oleo)

Mix above in small bowl.

Spread ½ of batter in 9 x 13-inch greased and floured pan.

Sprinkle ⅔ cup of the crumbs over the batter.

Pour the remaining batter over the crumbs. Top with remaining crumbs.

Bake 30-40 minutes.

## LAURA JONES, RETAIL MANAGER
Mount Rushmore Bookstores

# Buttermilk Blueberry Muffins

I once dreamed of owning and operating a bed & breakfast. Now my bed & breakfast is only at "home" with family and friends!

2 cups unbleached flour

2 tsp baking powder

½ tsp baking soda

⅓–½ cup sugar (less to more sweet)

1 cup buttermilk (the real secret to great-tasting muffins)

⅓ cup canola oil

1 egg

1 cup fresh or frozen blueberries

Cinnamon-sugar, optional

Preheat oven to 400°.

Spray two muffin tins (to make one dozen) with non-stick cooking spray or use paper muffin liners.

Mix dry ingredients in a small bowl and set aside.

Mix wet ingredients in a large bowl, except for blueberries.

Add dry ingredients to wet ingredients and mix just until blended (20 strokes). The batter will be lumpy! Don't over-mix or your muffins will be tough.

Gently mix in blueberries.

Fill muffin tins ⅔ full.

Sprinkle with cinnamon-sugar (optional).

Bake for 20 minutes. Muffins should be golden brown.

Cool slightly and gently remove from muffin tins.

Enjoy and just try not to eat the entire dozen in one sitting!

This recipe may be used with other berries as well. Raspberries and blackberries work well, too.

CHERYL A. SCHREIER, SUPERINTENDENT
Mount Rushmore National Memorial

# Cornbread

This is a very sweet and moist cornbread.

1 cup flour

1 cup cornmeal

⅔ cup sugar

1 tsp salt

3½ tsp baking powder

1 egg

1 cup milk

⅓ cup oil

⅓ cup sour cream

Mix all ingredients well and pour in an 8 x 8-inch pan.

Bake at 400° for 20 minutes.

ANNA RAUE, EXECUTIVE ADMINISTRATIVE ASSISTANT
Mount Rushmore Society

# *Appetizers*

## BADLANDS NATIONAL PARK

The rugged beauty of the Badlands draws visitors from around the world with its sharply eroded buttes, pinnacles and spires. These striking geologic deposits contain one of the world's richest fossil beds. Ancient mammals such as the rhino, horse and saber-toothed cat once roamed here. The park's 244,000 acres protect an expanse of mixed-grass prairie where bison, bighorn sheep, prairie dogs and black-footed ferrets live today.

LOCATED NEAR WALL, SD
Supported by Badlands Natural History Association

*"I had never seen anything which impressed so strongly on my mind a feeling of desolation . . . The wind was high and bleak; the barren, arid country seemed as if it had been swept by fires, and in every direction the same dull ash-colored hue derived from the formation met the eye . . . We left the place with pleasure." —John Fremont, diary 1842*

Black-footed ferrets live and
thrive in Badlands National Park.

# Cowboy Caviar

1 can (15 oz) black beans, drained

1 can (15 oz) black-eyed peas, drained

1 can (15 oz) diced tomatoes, drained

1 can (15 oz) whole kernel corn, drained

½ medium onion, minced

¼ cup green pepper, diced

½ cup green chilies, diced

½ tsp garlic salt

1 cup Italian dressing

¾ cup fresh cilantro, chopped

Mix and chill. Serve with tortilla chips or Scoops®.

EILEEN DIXON FLEISHACKER
Mount Rushmore Society

# Crappy* Tortilla Chip Dip

*This dish is so named because it is so easy and people love it. My husband started calling it "crappy dip" so no one else at parties would eat it, and he'd have it all to himself!

1  pkg (8oz) cream cheese, softened

1  cup medium salsa

2  cups shredded cheese (cheddar Jack or Mexican blend)

Beat cream cheese and salsa until smooth.

Spread in serving dish.

Top generously with shredded cheese.

Gently press cheese into the dip.

Chill until set. Serve with tortilla chips.

DAWN MILLER
Garretson, SD

# Warm Italiano Spread

This was originally a camping recipe. It was originally in a cast iron skillet with a lid. Very unusual taste and popular with guys!

1   pkg (8 oz) Neufchatel cheese

¼   cup pesto

1   large plum tomato, chopped

¼   cup shredded Italian 5-cheese

Layer on an oiled 8-inch piece of foil in a skillet or pie pan.

Cover with lid or foil tent. Grill 8-10 minutes on medium heat with cover down.

Serve with Pepper/Olive Oil Triscuits.

RUTH SAMUELSEN
Mount Rushmore Society


# Lemon Veggie Dip

This great summer dip has a light, bright flavor.

2   cups sour cream

1   cup grated pecorino or parmesan cheese

Zest or peel of one lemon

Mix and chill.

Serve with fresh veggies or crackers.

PAM LANG
Mount Rushmore Society

# BLT Dip

1   jar (3 oz) of real bacon pieces (NOT Bacos) OR 6 strips of crispy bacon, crumbled

1   cup sour cream

1   cup mayonnaise (not Miracle Whip)

1   cup tomatoes, diced

Combine all and chill for at least 1 hour.

Serve with crackers. Keebler's Bistro Cornbread crackers are the best for this dip.

DAWN MILLER
Garretson, SD

# Cheryl's Appetizer

4 cups shredded cheddar cheese

2 cups mayonnaise

1 cup chopped pecans

4 slices bacon, cooked and crumbled

1 bunch green onions, sliced

½ tsp seasoned salt

1 tsp pepper

Mix well and put in a spring-form pan. You can line the pan with Saran Wrap so it can be transferred to a plate easily.

Chill at least 1 hour.

Top with Hot Pepper Raspberry Preserves (available at specialty food stores).

Sprinkle shredded cilantro over it, if desired.

Serve with Triscuits.

COOK'S NOTE: I have a half spring-form pan (about 8 or 9 inches in diameter), and I usually make half of this recipe, as it goes a long way.

RUTH SAMUELSEN
Mount Rushmore Society

# Unique Olive Cheese Spread

1   pkg (8 oz) cream cheese, softened

½   cup mayonnaise

1   cup green olives, chopped in food processor

2   T olive juice

½   cup pecans, chopped

    Dash of pepper

Combine all ingredients and mix well.

Chill at least 2 hours before serving.

Serve with a variety of crackers.

JODY KETEL
Mount Rushmore Society

# Meatballs

3 lb ground beef

½ cup onion, chopped

1 can (12 oz) evaporated milk

½ tsp garlic powder

1 cup oatmeal

2 tsp chili powder

1 cup cracker crumbs

2 tsp salt

2 eggs

½ tsp pepper

Mix all ingredients.

Freeze.

Makes 80 walnut-sized meatballs.

## TO MAKE BBQ MEATBALLS

2 cups catsup

½ tsp liquid smoke

1 cup brown sugar

½ tsp garlic powder

¼ cup onion, chopped

Top meatballs with sauce. Bake at 350° for 1 hour.

## PATTY CHILDERS
Badlands National Park

# Stuffed Jalapeños

I grow jalapeño peppers to make jelly and save the large ones for this recipe!

22  large fresh jalapeños, cut in half lengthwise and scoop out.

FILLING

1  lb Italian sausage, browned, drained and crumbled

1  pkg (8 oz) cream cheese

4  oz shredded Parmesan

Stuff prepared filling into peppers (in a greased pan).

Sprinkle with Mexican cheese or your cheese choice.

Bake at 425° for 15-20 minutes. Serve hot.

RUTH SAMUELSEN
Mount Rushmore Society

## EDIBLE CENTERPIECE

This looks great in the center of a veggie platter.

1  pineapple top (remove some of the center leaves)

3  halves of small zucchinis (flat side out)

3  ends of whole carrots (about 2 inches long)

6  slices of large radishes

6  halves of black olives

Cut the carrots for beaks.

Attach zucchinis.

Add "eyes" as shown. Use toothpicks to attach.

# Mom's Pickled Eggs

1½ cups cider vinegar

¼ tsp liquid smoke

½ cup water

1 tsp pickling spice

2 tsp salt

2 T brown sugar

1 dozen boiled eggs, peeled

Mix vinegar, water, salt, liquid smoke, pickling spice and brown sugar.

Bring to a boil and then simmer for 5 minutes.

Pour over the dozen peeled eggs in a glass jar container.

Let stand in the refrigerator for 2 days at least before eating. They get better with age!

ECHO BOHL
Devils Tower Natural History Association

# Laura's Make-Ahead Meatballs

4 eggs

2 cups dried bread crumbs

1 tsp salt

½ cup onion, chopped

½ tsp pepper

4 lb ground beef, browned

2 tsp Worcestershire sauce

Beat eggs well.

Stir in all of remaining ingredients except ground beef. Mix well.

Then mix in ground beef.

Shape into 1-inch meatballs.

Bake at 400° for 10–15 minutes.

Drain, cool and freeze.

Yield: 12 dozen

PATTY CHILDERS
Badlands National Park

Yellowstone National Park

# *Soups & Salads*

## NATIONAL PARK SERVICE

Since 1916, the National Park Service has been entrusted to care for America's national parks. With the help of volunteers and park partners, the organization preserves more than 400 parks, monuments, historic sites and memorials so their stories are forever told.

# Waldorf Salad

A favorite of President Franklin D. Roosevelt served during a Mount Rushmore dinner in 2010.

2   large sweet apples, sliced

½   cup raisins

1   cup celery, sliced thin

1   cup walnut or pecan pieces

6   T mayonnaise

Sprinkle apple slices with lemon juice to keep them from darkening.

Mix all ingredients with mayonnaise and chill.

Yield: 5-6 servings

# Spaghetti Salad

1   box spaghetti noodles, drained

2   tomatoes, diced

1   green pepper, diced

1   onion, chopped and grated

1   large bottle Viva Italian Dressing or any zesty Italian dressing

Mix together and season with Salad Supreme Seasoning.

You can play with this and add colorful veggies, olives, salami, cheese chunks, etc.

JUDY DUHAMEL
Mount Rushmore Society

# Harlequin Salad

A favorite of President John Adams and served during a Mount Rushmore dinner in 2008.

| | |
|---|---|
| 1 | cup red cabbage |
| 1 | cup green cabbage |
| 1 | cup peas |
| ½ | cup beets |
| 1 | onion, diced |
| ½ | cup carrots, diced |
| | Salt and pepper |
| | French dressing |

Shave cabbage thin.

Separately cook peas, beets and carrots till tender. Drain and chill.

Mix all vegetables or arrange them in layers or heaps. The effect is better if they are mixed.

Pour on French dressing 1 hour before serving. Keep cold.

Pass more French dressing at the table.

Yield: 4-6 servings

# Spinach and Walnut Salad with Warm Bleu Cheese Dressing

1   cup golden raisins, plumped in warm water and drained

6   cups baby spinach leaves

1   cup walnut pieces, lightly toasted

1   Granny Smith apple, thinly sliced

1   cup bleu cheese, crumbled

1⅓  cups milk

2   T extra virgin olive oil

    Salt and freshly ground black pepper to taste

3   tsp cornstarch

Arrange spinach on 4 plates and top with walnuts, raisins, apple slices and 6 T of bleu cheese.

Combine milk, oil and remaining cheese in small sauce pan over low heat until cheese melts.

Season with salt and pepper.

Whisk in cornstarch 1 tsp at a time until dressing thickens.

Dress each salad liberally with warm dressing.

EILEEN DIXON FLEISHACKER
Mount Rushmore Society

**Grand Teton National Park**

# Buckwheat Noodles with Asparagus in Sesame Dressing

This is a great potluck dish, as it is served at room temperature.

- 1 lb soba noodles, boiled until just al dente. (You can use whole wheat linguine and break in half.)
- 1 lb asparagus, cooked until crisp
- 6 green onions, cut into ¼-inch pieces

## DRESSING

- 1 cup soy sauce
- ¼ cup chicken stock or broth
- 1 T sugar
- 3 T sesame seeds, toasted in small skillet. Reserve 1½ T for garnish.

Blend or shake in jar. Set aside.

Drain noodles and toss with dressing. It looks pretty soupy, but the noodles will absorb the liquid.

Cool.

Plunge asparagus in ice water, then drain. Cut diagonally into 1-inch pieces.

Reserve some of the tips for garnish.

Add to pasta, along with green onions.

Garnish with remaining sesame seeds and asparagus.

Serve at room temperature.

Yield: 12 servings

RUTH SAMUELSEN
Mount Rushmore Society

# Chicken Salad

4 cups cooked chicken breasts, cut in chunks

1 can (15 oz) pineapple chunks, drained

1 cup celery, chopped

1 large can mandarin oranges

1 T onion, chopped

1 cup whole grapes, any color

1 cup walnuts, coarsely chopped

1 can chow mien noodles

1 cup mayonnaise

1 T mustard

Garlic salt to taste

Mix all together.

Can all be mixed ahead (except for noodles) or just before serving.

JUDY DUHAMEL
Mount Rushmore Society

# Wild Rice Salad

½ lb wild rice (about 1½ cups), rinsed

Boil in 5 cups salted water, uncovered, for about 40 minutes, until tender. Drain and transfer to a bowl to cool. Chill covered until cold for about 2 hours.

## IN A LARGE BOWL, COMBINE

2 celery ribs, chopped

2 small tomatoes, seeded and chopped

½ carrot, diced in ¼-inch pieces

½ green pepper, diced in ¼-inch pieces

½ yellow bell pepper, diced in ¼-inch pieces

½ cup sliced almonds, toasted

½ cup raisins, craisins or dried cherries

Toss with wild rice.

## DRESSING

6 T Balsamic vinegar

3 T vegetable oil

1 tsp minced garlic

Salt and pepper to taste

Whisk together.

Toss well. Seal and chill. Can be made 2 days ahead.

Yield: 6-8 servings

## RUTH SAMUELSEN
Mount Rushmore Society

# Swift Strawberry Salad

This is a great light dish for any occasion.

    4   cups strawberries, sliced
    1   T caramel ice cream topping
    2   T maple syrup
    1   T orange juice
    ⅓   cup cashews or other nuts

Place berries in serving bowl.

Combine caramel, syrup and orange juice. Drizzle over berries.

Just before serving, sprinkle nuts over the top.

DAWN MILLER
Garretson, SD

# The Family's Favorite Cherry Salad

    1   can cherry pie mix
    1   can crushed pineapple, drained
    1   can sweetened condensed milk
    1   carton (8 oz) Cool Whip, slightly softened
    ½   pkg miniature marshmallows

Fold all ingredients together in large bowl.

Refrigerate until serving. It also freezes very well.

Optional additions: mandarin oranges, coconut, walnuts or pecans.

EVELYN BACHMEIER
Rapid City, SD

# Shirley's Orange Fluff

1   cup water

1   cup milk

1   large pkg orange Jello

1   pkg tapioca pudding (not instant)

Combine and bring to a boil. Cook over medium heat until it starts to thicken.

Remove from heat and refrigerate until it is just barely warm.

ADD

1   can crushed pineapple, drained

1   can mandarin oranges, drained

1   carton (12 oz) Cool Whip

Stir, chill and serve.

SHIRLEY BAKER
Mankato, MN

# Pat's Perfect Potato Salad

In memory of Patricia Jonason Nielsen. My first memories of parks included Jonason family reunions at Lewis and Clark Recreation Area. Mom's carefully chilled potato salad was always a hit. The cooked dressing is the key.

DRESSING

|       |                                                              |
|-------|--------------------------------------------------------------|
| 4     | eggs, beaten                                                 |
| 2½ T  | prepared mustard (the better the mustard, the better the dressing!) |
| ¾ cup | sugar                                                        |
| ½ cup | vinegar                                                      |

Combine ingredients and cook over low heat, stirring constantly. Mixture will thicken like a pudding.

Set aside and cool.

Add 1 cup mayonnaise, or Miracle Whip for sweeter dressing.

Mix well.

Dressing will keep for one week.

|        |                                                                      |
|--------|----------------------------------------------------------------------|
| 8-10   | hard-boiled eggs, peeled and chopped                                 |
| 3 lb   | potatoes, boiled, peeled and diced (It's OK to leave some peel on, though!) |
| ¼ cup  | mild onion, chopped                                                  |
| ¼ cup  | celery, chopped                                                      |
| ¼ cup  | green or red pepper, chopped                                         |

Mix all together and chill.

Yield: 8-10 servings

DIANA NIELSEN SAATHOFF, EXECUTIVE DIRECTOR
Mount Rushmore Society

# Ham & Hash Brown Soup

2½  cups water

2  cups frozen hash browns, cubed

2  cups ham, cubed

½  cups carrots, thinly sliced

½  cup green peppers, chopped

¼  cup sweet red pepper, chopped

1  can (15 oz) can cream style corn

1  can (11 oz) can nacho fiesta soup

½  cup water

Pepper to taste

Combine first 6 ingredients in Dutch oven. Bring to a boil. Cover, reduce heat and simmer 15 minutes or until vegetables are tender. Add remaining ingredients. Cook until thoroughly heated, stirring often.

DAWN MILLER
Garretson, SD

**Minuteman Missile Historic Site**

# Black Bean Soup

Black Bean Soup is actually a soup that is almost a stew.

| | |
|---|---|
| 2 T extra virgin olive oil | 3 cans (15 ozs) black beans |
| 1 dried bay leaf | 2 T ground cumin |
| 1 jalapeño pepper, seeded and chopped | 1½ tsp ground coriander |
| 4 garlic cloves, chopped (add extra) | Salt and fresh pepper |
| 3 celery tips with greens, chopped | 2–3 T plus 2 tsp hot sauce |
| 1 large onion, chopped | 1 quart chicken or vegetable broth |
| 1 red bell pepper, cored, seeded and chopped | 1 can (15 oz) diced tomatoes |
| | Sour cream and scallions (optional) |

Heat medium soup pot over medium heat. Add olive oil to hot pot, then add bay leaves, jalapenos, garlic, celery and onions.

Cook for 3½ minutes.

Then add bell peppers and continue to cook. Drain 2 cans beans and add.

With remaining can, pour the juice and ½ of beans into pot.

Use a fork to mash up the remaining beans in the can.

Stir the mashed beans into the pot and season with the cumin, coriander, salt, pepper and ⅔ T of the hot sauce.

Add the stock and tomatoes to the soup and bring to a bubble.

Reduce heat and simmer for 15 minutes over low heat.

Top soup with sour cream and scallions.

JUDY DUHAMEL
Mount Rushmore Society

# Clam Chowder

    1   cup water

    1   can (8 oz) minced clams with juice

    1   chicken bouillon cube

    2   cups diced potatoes

    2   cups carrots, thinly sliced

1½   cups minced onions

    1   tsp chopped parsley

Cook above mixture until veggies are done.

ADD

    1   can cream of celery soup

    2   cups milk

2½   tsp seasoning salt

    8   oz shredded cheese (Jack or mixture of Jack and cheddar)

    ¼   cup cooking sherry (optional)

Cook gently to heat and melt cheese.

Cooking sherry can be added if desired.

Serve with warm, crusty bread.

SUE SKROVE
Devils Tower National Monument

# The Famous Senate Restaurant Bean Soup Recipe

A favorite of President Harry S. Truman and served at a Mount Rushmore dinner in 2011.

| | |
|---|---|
| 2 | lb dried navy beans |
| 4 | qt hot water |
| 1½ | lbs smoked ham hocks |
| 1 | onion, chopped |
| 2 | T butter |
| | Salt and pepper to taste |

Wash the navy beans and run hot water through them until they are slightly whitened.

Place beans into pot with hot water.

Add ham hocks and simmer approximately 3 hours in a covered pot, stirring occasionally.

Remove ham hocks and set aside to cool.

Dice meat and return to soup.

Lightly brown the onion in butter.

Add to soup.

Before serving, bring to a boil and season with salt and pepper.

Yield: 9 servings

# Potato Sausage Soup

  ½  lb Italian sausage

  ½  lb turkey sausage

  1  large onion, chopped

Brown and drain.

ADD

  1  pkg (16 oz) frozen hash browns

  1  can (14 oz) chicken broth

  2  cups water

  1  can cream of celery soup

  1  can cream of chicken soup

  2  cups milk

Cook on low in crock pot all day.

JUDY DUHAMEL
Mount Rushmore Society

**Fort Laramie Historic Site**

# Mushroom Barley Beef Soup

1-1½  lb stew meat, with visible fat removed
        and cut into bite-size pieces

    1  T oil

    2  cups onions, chopped

    1  cup carrots, diced

    ½  cup celery, diced

1-2  cups mushrooms, sliced

    1  tsp garlic or 1 clove, minced

    ¼  tsp dried thyme

    1  can or 2 cups beef broth

    1  can or 2 cups chicken broth

    2  cups water

    ½  cup pearl barley

    ¾  tsp salt

    ¼  tsp pepper

Brown stew meat in oil.

Add vegetables and cook until soft.

Add mushrooms, garlic, thyme, broths, water, barley and seasonings.

Bring to a boil, reduce heat, cover and simmer 1 ½ hours.

Garnish with parsley.

Ladle into bowls and serve.

May also be made in crock pot after browning meat. Add rest of ingredients to pot and cook on low for 8-10 hours.

JODY DAVILA
Wind Cave National Park

# Pheasant & Creamy Wild Rice Soup

This is one of the most delicious soups we have ever tasted. I got the recipe from the Dakota Wesleyan University president's wife over 20 years ago.

| | | | |
|---|---|---|---|
| 8 | strips thick-sliced bacon, diced | 6 | cups half & half |
| 2⅔ | cups wild rice, uncooked | 1 | cup butter, softened |
| 1½ | cups onion, diced | 1½ | cups flour |
| 1½ | cups celery, diced | 1 | tsp salt |
| 1½ | cups carrots, diced | ½ | tsp white or black pepper |
| 1½ | qt (6 cups) water | 3 | cups cooked pheasant, diced |
| 3 | qt chicken broth, hot | | |

Fry bacon. Drain and reserve ½ cup of fat.

Saute onion, rice, carrots and celery in fat for 5 minutes.

Place bacon and sautéed veggies in large cooking vessel and stir in 4 cups (1 qt) of the hot broth.

Heat, stirring constantly, until the soup thickens and bubbles, about 1 minute.

Add the rest of the half & half, the water and broth.

Stir in the salt, pepper and pheasant.

Season more to taste.

This serves 40, so I always freeze some. It re-heats beautifully!

Serve with chopped parsley on top.

JODY KETEL
Mount Rushmore Society

# Tortilla Soup

1    medium onion, chopped

2    garlic cloves, minced

2    T vegetable oil

1    can (14 oz) diced tomatoes (with juice)

1    can (10½ oz) condensed beef broth

1    can (10½ oz) condensed chicken broth

1    can (10½ oz) condensed tomato soup

1    cup water

½    cup salsa

2    tsp Worcestershire sauce

1    tsp ground cumin

1    tsp chili powder

8    corn tortillas, cut into wedges

½    cup shredded cheddar cheese

Cook onion and garlic in oil in Dutch oven until tender but not brown. Drain well.

Add other ingredients except tortillas and cheese.

Bring to a boil and reduce heat.

Simmer uncovered 1 hour.

Add tortillas and continue to simmer 10 minutes.

Ladle into soup bowls and sprinkle with cheese.

Yield: 9 cups

For a heartier soup, add 1 can (12 oz) white chicken breast when adding the tortillas.

JODY DAVILA
Wind Cave National Park

# 6 Hour Stew

2  lb stew beef (or cut up any roast, such as arm roast)

    Potatoes

    Onions

    Carrots

1  large can whole tomatoes

2  T tapioca

    Salt and pepper

1  piece bread, cut into cubes

½  cup red wine

Put tomatoes through blender, if you like.

Place all ingredients into large covered casserole dish.

Cook 5-6 hours at 175-300°. DO NOT UNCOVER DURING COOKING TIME.

JUDY DUHAMEL
Mount Rushmore Society

# Broccoli-Ham Soup

This is a good low-cal recipe to use leftover broccoli and ham. Quick too!

¼ cup onion, chopped

3 T margarine

¼ cup all-purpose flour

1½ tsp instant chicken bouillon granules

1 tsp ground mustard

½ tsp dried thyme, crushed

⅛ tsp pepper

2 cups skim milk

2 cups water

2 cups broccoli florets or frozen cut broccoli

1½ cups fully cooked ham, cubed

In a 3-quart saucepan, cook the onion in margarine until tender, but not browned.

Stir in flour, chicken bouillon granules, mustard, thyme and pepper.

Add milk and water all at once.

Cook and stir over medium heat until thick and bubbly.

Stir in broccoli and ham.

Return to boiling.

Reduce heat and simmer for 4–6 minutes more until broccoli is tender and soup is heated through, stirring occasionally.

Yield: 4 servings

JODY DAVILA
Wind Cave National Park

Theodore Roosevelt National Park

**BADLANDS NATURAL HISTORY ASSOCIATION:** Founded in 1959, Badlands Natural History Association is a not-for-profit organization established to support education and research efforts at Badlands National Park. The profits from bookstore sales are used to support the park newspaper, intern program, library, photographic collections and the Artist-In-Residence program.

**DEVILS TOWER NATURAL HISTORY ASSOCIATION:** First established in 1958, Devils Tower Natural History Association is a not-for-profit corporation incorporated under the laws of the State of Wyoming. Its mission is to promote understanding and conservation of the natural, cultural and historical resources of the monument through education, public information and service.

**MOUNT RUSHMORE BOOKSTORES:**
As a committee of the Mount Rushmore Society and established in 1993, the mission of the Mount Rushmore Bookstores is to support education and interpretation of Mount Rushmore National Memorial by funding seasonal rangers, the Junior Ranger program, cultural programs and other activities.

**BLACK HILLS PARKS & FORESTS ASSOCIATION:** This organization is a non-profit cooperating arm of the National Park Service, National Forest Service, South Dakota Game, Fish & Parks and National Grasslands. It operates sales outlets in 14 locations throughout the Black Hills and the Nebraska Panhandle. Purchases from sites support interpretive programming at many locations.

*Entrées*

## MOUNT RUSHMORE NATIONAL MEMORIAL

When sculptor Gutzon Borglum looked upon the knobby, cracked face of Mount Rushmore in the Black Hills of South Dakota, he saw a vision of four United States presidents carved into the mountain. Between 1927 and 1941, with the help of over 400 workers and several influential politicians, Borglum carved a memorial to the history of America. Presidents George Washington, Thomas Jefferson, Theodore Roosevelt and Abraham Lincoln represent the birth, growth, preservation and development of the nation.

**LOCATED NEAR KEYSTONE, SD**
**Supported by Mount Rushmore Society**

*"... Hence, let us place there, carved high, as close to heaven as we can, the words of our leaders, their faces, to show posterity what manner of men they were."—Gutzon Borglum*

**Rocky Mountain goat**

# Momma Millie's Biftek Miramonde

1 pkg small noodles, cooked and drained

Parmesan cheese

## CHEESE FILLING

1 carton (16 ozs) sour cream

1 pkg (8 oz) cream cheese, room temperature

1 carton (16 ozs) cottage cheese

Mix together.

## MEAT SAUCE

1½ lb ground beef

1 small can tomato paste

½ tsp dried thyme

1 medium can tomato sauce

1 bay leaf

1 can tomatoes

½ tsp oregano

2 medium onions, chopped

3 cloves garlic, minced

1 bell pepper, chopped

Salt and pepper to taste

1 cup celery, chopped

1 small jar mushrooms, cut up

Cook meat sauce like spaghetti sauce.

Put noodles in bottom of large, round casserole dish.

Make nest in middle and add the cheese mixture.

Place meat sauce over all and sprinkle with Parmesan cheese.

Bake at 325° for 25 minutes.

Serve with salad and French bread.

*"I love the national parks because of their capacity to heal us, to delight us, to bring us to awe and to educate us. They are indeed one of the best ideas we Americans have ever had and realized."*

## RENEE CARRIER
Devils Tower Natural History Association

# Pepper & Ginger BBQ Ribs

1 cup ketchup

2 T Worcestershire sauce

1 tsp onion powder

1 tsp garlic powder

2 tsp white pepper (or 1 tsp cayenne)

2 tsp ginger powder

2 lbs ribs, beef or pork

1 tsp salt

1 beer

Open beer; pour into pint glass and drink.

Trim excess fat from ribs and place in stock pot. Completely cover ribs with water. Add salt to water to help prevent boiling over. Boil at medium roll for 40 minutes. Skim off foam.

While ribs boil, mix together first 6 ingredients (through ginger) in bowl and whisk until smooth.

Pull ribs from water and place on clean dish towel to cool.

Start grill and set to low or start broiler on low and place wire rack on 2nd tier from top of oven. Coat ribs with sauce mixture and grill directly over heat until sauce darkens at contact spots. If using broiler, place foil at bottom of broiler pan to help with cleanup. Spray top of broiler with cooking spray or light coat of oil brushed on to prevent sticking. Place broiler on wire rack and broil to point where sauce darkens. If it blackens a bit, that's okay, too!

Flip ribs and slather with more BBQ sauce and cook until you get the grill marks desired.

Pull ribs from heat, get another beer and repeat step 1. Call the carnivores. Dinner is served!

COOK'S NOTE: Reduce white pepper to 1 tsp for milder sauce or add 2 T of your favorite bottled BBQ sauce to the mix for a touch of your favorite flavor. Abraham Lincoln was known to be fond of ginger, especially in cookies!

ROXANNE HORKEY, ASSISTANT
RETAIL MANAGER
Xanterra Parks & Resorts

# Hamburger Goulash

1   lb ground beef

1   Irish potato, peeled and cubed

1   onion, peeled and cubed

1   cabbage, cut into thin slices*

    Soy sauce

    Salt & pepper to taste

In large skillet or pot, crumble ground beef and add a cup or so of water.

Bring to a boil and add potatoes, onions, salt, pepper and soy sauce to taste.

When the potatoes are done, add cabbage and cook until just crispy tender.

Serve over rice.

*In place of cabbage, you might add green beans and mushrooms or a combination of beans, cabbage and mushrooms. Makes a nice one-dish meal.

*"I love our national parks because they're kept intact, preserved for us to enjoy and appreciate. They are just special to our precious USA!"*

JUNE CRUMLEY
Ramrod Key, FL

# Linda's Party Sandwiches

1½  lb hamburger, cooked and drained

1  chopped onion, browned and drained

## TURN HEAT TO LOW AND ADD

1  lb Velveeta, cubed

1  small can tomato sauce

1  small can chopped black olives

½  tsp chile powder

At this point you can serve on buns or put into party buns.

Wrap each in foil.

Bake at 350° for 15-20 minutes.

Yield: 24 sandwiches

RUTH SAMUELSEN
Mount Rushmore Society

# Chicken Breasts Diane

Wide egg noodles, cooked and drained

4 large boneless and skinless chicken breast halves or 8 small ones

½ tsp salt

¼–½ tsp black pepper

2 T olive oil

2 T butter

3 T chives, chopped

3 T parsley, chopped

Juice of ½ lime or lemon

2 T brandy or red wine

2 tsp Dijon-style mustard

¼ cup chicken broth

Place chicken breast halves between sheets of waxed paper or plastic wrap.

Pound slightly with mallet.

Sprinkle with salt and pepper.

Heat 1 tablespoon each of oil and butter in large skillet

Cook chicken over high heat for 3 minutes on each side. Do not cook longer or they will be overcooked and dry.

Transfer to warm serving platter.

Add chives, lemon or lime juice, wine or brandy, parsley and mustard to pan.

Cook 15 seconds, whisking constantly.

Whisk in broth.

Stir until sauce is smooth.

Whisk in remaining butter and oil.

Pour sauce over chicken.

Serve over hot wide egg noodles.

Yield: 4 servings

LYNN BAUTER, FINANCE DIRECTOR
Mount Rushmore Society

# Colorado Chicken

| | | | |
|---|---|---|---|
| 6 | chicken breasts | 4 | cloves garlic, coarsely chopped |
| 2 | cups sour cream | 4 | tsp salt |
| ¼ | cup lemon juice | ½ | tsp pepper |
| 4 | tsp Worcestershire sauce | ½ | cup butter |
| 4 | tsp celery salt | ½ | cup shortening |
| 2 | tsp paprika | 1¾ | cups fine breadcrumbs |

Preheat over to 350°.

Combine everything except chicken, butter, shortening and bread crumbs.

Mix well.

Add chicken, making sure to coat well.

Marinate overnight (or at least a few hours; the longer the better).

Drain chicken, coat with breadcrumbs.

Melt butter and shortening.

Spoon ¾ cup over chicken.

Bake 45 minutes.

Spoon remaining butter/shortening mix on chicken.

Bake an additional 15 minutes.

DAWN MILLER
Garretson, SD

# Never-Fail Cheesy Rice Casserole

1 cup wild or slow-cooking rice (pre-cook ½ hour if using wild rice)

1 can (14 oz) tomatoes, diced

1 pkg (4 oz) Velveeta cheese, cubed

1 medium onion, diced

½ cup olive oil

1 can (4 oz) sliced mushrooms, drained

½ cup sliced black olives

1 tsp salt

1½ cups water, boiling

Place all ingredients in casserole, except water.

When ready to bake, add water.

Bake uncovered at 350° for 1½ hours, stirring occasionally.

This recipe can be made and refrigerated ahead of time.

BONNY (BRAY) ARMACOST
Hillsborough, California

# Pasta with Sausage and Broccoli

1 lb ground hot Italian sausage

2 tsp minced garlic

12 oz rotelle pasta

1 large bunch broccoli or frozen cuts

¾ cup grated Parmesan cheese

Bring a large pot of water to a boil.

Meanwhile, brown sausage in a large skillet over medium-high heat, stirring often to break up clumps. Reduce heat to low, stir in garlic and cover to keep warm.

Add pasta to the boiling water and cook according to package directions, adding broccoli for the last 4 minutes cooking time.

Remove and reserve ½ cup pasta cooking water.

Drain pasta and pour into a serving bowl.

Add sausage, reserved cooking water and ½ cup of the Parmesan cheese.

Toss to mix.

Serve with remaining cheese.

LYNN BAUTER, FINANCE DIRECTOR
Mount Rushmore Society

# Cilantro Lime Chicken

4   boneless chicken breasts

4   limes

1   T lime zest

4   cloves garlic, halved

   Fresh cilantro, chopped

   Shredded cheese (optional)

In a plastic bag, combine juice of 3 limes, zest, garlic and roughly ½ cup cilantro.

Mix well and add chicken.

Chill for 1-2 hours.

Grill or broil.

To serve, top with shredded cheese (if desired) and squeeze lime juice over.

Serve with Spanish rice.

DAWN MILLER
Garretson, SD

# Crusted Cheddar Chicken Breasts

This is a delicious comfort food. The combination of the salad mustard, sour cream and cheddar cheese makes for a delightful aromatic taste. You may also substitute cheeses and mustard so as to be able to add any other combinations of taste your heart may desire.

Boneless, skinless chicken breasts

## COMBINE IN MEDIUM BOWL UNTIL SMOOTH

| | |
|---|---|
| 2 oz sour cream | ¾ cup milk |
| 2 oz salad mustard | 1 tsp dry mustard |

## COMBINE IN SMALL BOWL

| | |
|---|---|
| 3 oz bread crumbs, finely chopped and dried | 2 oz melted butter or margarine |

## ADD TO CRUMBS

2 oz sharp cheddar cheese, finely grated

1 oz cheddar/white blend cheese, finely grated.

Dip each chicken breast in the mustard blend and let the excess liquid run off.

Lay the breast on the cheese-bread crumb blend.

Sprinkle the blend on the top of the chicken breast.

Then place the breast on a lightly greased sheet pan.

Repeat for all chicken breasts.

Bake for 11 minutes in a convection oven. Rotate and bake for another 11 minutes or until the internal temperature of the chicken breasts is 165°.

*"I can think of no other place on earth where I would rather earn my living than in a national park. It lets me see the lesson of life displayed in all its' beauty."*

ROGER FLANAGAN, CHEF
Xanterra Parks & Resorts

# Bucky's Chili

1   lb hamburger, browned

½   lb Hillshire Farm Smoked Sausage, cut in ¼-inch slices

4   strips bacon, cooked and crumbled

2   cans (15 oz) of mild chili beans

1   can (15 oz) red kidney beans

1   can (15 oz) petite diced tomatoes

1   can (12 oz) tomato sauce

2   cans (6 oz) mild diced green chilies

1   medium onion, diced

½   jar medium picante sauce

1   pkg mild Schilling chili mix

2   cloves minced garlic

1   tsp chili powder

1   tsp garlic

    Salt and pepper

2½   cups water

Combine all ingredients in large cooking pot and simmer 2-3 hours.

Serve with Fritos and shredded cheese.

**BOB MUDLIN, PRESIDENT**
Presidential Parking, Inc.

# Berdell's Meat Loaf

Berdell was a good friend, fellow realtor and a great chef who, unfortunately, is no longer with us. She also was the owner of a local bed and breakfast, and this recipe was one of her favorites. I have prepared it many times since she shared it with me. Everyone raves!

| | | | |
|---|---|---|---|
| ¾ | cup milk | ¼ | tsp pepper |
| ¾ | cup crushed saltines | ½ | tsp allspice |
| 2 | lb lean ground beef | ½ | tsp sage |
| 1 | onion, minced | 2 | T shredded Parmesan |
| 1 | tsp salt | | |

Soak the crushed saltines in the milk for 5 minutes.

In a separate bowl, mix everything else together except for the ground beef.

Then, put it all together and knead.

Form into a meat loaf and put in a pan.

## TOPPING

| | | | |
|---|---|---|---|
| 6 | T brown sugar | ½ | cup ketchup |
| ½ | tsp nutmeg | 2 | tsp dry mustard |

Whisk together well.

Put on top of the meat loaf.

Bake at 350° for 80-90 minutes.

Yield: 6 servings

ANDY KNIGHT, PRESIDENT
Mount Rushmore Society

# Gramma Sis' Savory Spaghetti Sauce

This recipe dates back to the 1950s and came from Shelbyville, IL. It is one of the few things Gramma Sis brought back to South Dakota from Illinois. She invested her inheritance of $50,000 in a dairy in Shelbyville that went broke and came back with this recipe and two kids. Uncle Jack told her the breeding fees in South Dakota were a heck of a lot less than in Illinois, but I think this recipe made up for it.

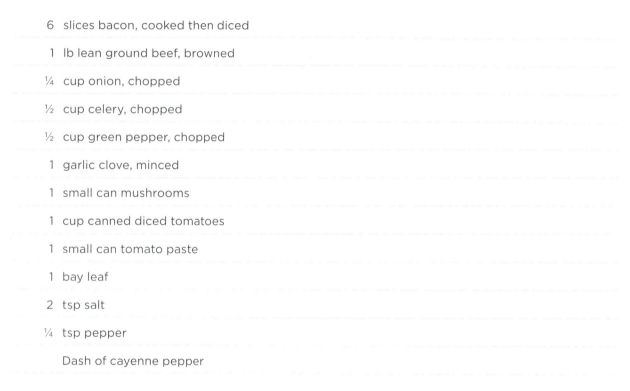

| | |
|---|---|
| 6 | slices bacon, cooked then diced |
| 1 | lb lean ground beef, browned |
| ¼ | cup onion, chopped |
| ½ | cup celery, chopped |
| ½ | cup green pepper, chopped |
| 1 | garlic clove, minced |
| 1 | small can mushrooms |
| 1 | cup canned diced tomatoes |
| 1 | small can tomato paste |
| 1 | bay leaf |
| 2 | tsp salt |
| ¼ | tsp pepper |
| | Dash of cayenne pepper |

Mix all together and simmer. The longer it simmers the better it gets. Pour over noodles, as desired. This recipe serves 4 pretty well. Just double or triple it—whatever works. You can never have too much left over.

JOHN & SUSAN CULBERSON
Black Hills Parks & Forests Association

# Hot Beef Sammies

Beef roast (any size)

1   can Coke (not diet)

1   pkg dry onion soup mix

Place beef in crockpot.

Pour Coke over roast.

Sprinkle with soup mix.

Slow cook until done, about 6-8 hours.

Fork shred and serve on buns.

DAWN MILLER
Garretson, SD

# Susan's Hot Chick(en) Dish

The kids always request this when they come home. It is a family favorite.

| | |
|---|---|
| 1 | bag taco chips |
| 1 | whole chicken, cooked then skinned and deboned |
| 1 | can cream of mushroom soup |
| 1 | can cream of chicken soup |
| ½ | cup onion, chopped |
| 1 | small container sour cream |
| | Jalapeño peppers to desired level of heat. We use 2-3 big peppers, and it is moderately hot |
| | Shredded sharp cheddar cheese |

Crush the chips and layer them into a 9 x 12-inch baking pan.

Layer in the chicken.

Mix together the soups, onion and jalapeños. It works better if the soup mixture is warmed up a bit before placing it in the pan.

Pour over chicken.

Sprinkle cheese over the top and place in a 325˚ oven for ½ hour to 45 minutes.

Put the pan on a top rack so the chips do not burn.

JOHN & SUSAN CULBERSON
Black Hills Parks & Forests Association

# Prime Steak Rub

1½  T kosher salt

1½  T brown sugar

1  tsp fresh cracked black pepper

½  tsp smoked paprika

½  tsp garlic powder

¼  tsp chili powder

¼  tsp cayenne

Mix thoroughly and rub on steaks.

Wrap tightly in plastic wrap.

Refrigerate at least 8 hours. Overnight or up to 2 days is best.

Grill.

Double the recipe and place any unused rub in an airtight container and freeze so it's ready

for the next barbeque.

DAWN MILLER
Garretson, SD

# Baked Trout with Parsley Stuffing

During the first presidential administration of Grover Cleveland (1885–1889), a recipe called "Baked Salmon Trout," made with parsley and cream, was served at the White House.

2   leeks, chopped fine (after removing root ends and darker green tops)

6   T butter

2½  cups regular or panko bread crumbs

½   cup parsley, minced fine

4   T lemon juice

2   tsp marjoram

    Salt and pepper

2   whole trout, with heads intact if possible

Heat oven to 400°.

Sauté leeks in 5 T of butter in skillet over medium heat until soft, 2-3 minutes.

Turn off heat, add bread crumbs, minced parsley, marjoram and 1 T of lemon juice.

Toss to mix well.

Lay trout in lightly oiled shallow baking dish.

Brush inside and outside of trout with remaining T of lemon juice; lightly salt and pepper. Spoon bread crumb mixture into body cavities. Some spill-out may occur. That's okay.

Melt remaining 1 T butter and drizzle over trout.

Cover loosely with foil and bake for 8 minutes.

Pull foil and bake for another 7 minutes. Flesh becomes slightly opaque at thickest part by tail and flakes easily when done.

Pull from oven, plate and serve with lemon wedges.

Cook's note: If using dried parsley and marjoram, add dried herbs in when sautéing leeks. Also add extra lemon juice or water to bread crumbs when mixing if it looks too dry.

ROXANNE HORKEY, ASSISTANT RETAIL MANAGER
Xanterra Parks & Resorts

# Salmon on a Cedar Plank

1   2 lb salmon filet, skin on

Soak cedar plank* in warm water for 20-30 minutes.

MIX

½   cup brown sugar

2   T canola oil

1   T dried thyme leaves

1   tsp (or less) cayenne pepper

Preheat grill to high and adjust to medium-low after 15 minutes.

Place the salmon, skin side down, on the plank.

Pat the dry mixture over the salmon.

Place plank and salmon on the grate and cook, with grill covered, about 20-35 minutes or just until the surface fat begins to turn white.

COOK'S NOTE: You can scrape and save the plank. You can also break it up and put it on coals on the grill for later flavoring. The dry mixture used here also makes a wonderful glaze.

*You must use a special cedar plank for grilling—NOT just a plank of cedar wood, as it is not safe.

RUTH SAMUELSEN
Mount Rushmore Society

# Herbed Pork Roast

6 lb loin of pork

2 carrots

2 onions

2 large cloves garlic

½ cup celery leaves

¼ cup parsley sprigs

4 whole cloves

3 bay leaves

1 can beef consommé

½ soup can of water

## RUB

3 tsp salt

1 tsp pepper

1 tsp thyme

½ tsp mace or nutmeg

Rub surface of meat with mixture.

Place meat with fat side up on rack in shallow open pan.

Roast uncovered at 400° for 20 minutes.

Lower temp to 350° and add rest of ingredients.

Baste and continue to cook until desired internal temp is reached.

SUE SKROVE
Devils Tower National Monument

# Eggplant Casserole

This dish is layered like lasagna, but without the noodles.

Thinly slice an eggplant width-wise in circles. Rinse, dry and season with a bit of salt. Bake slices in oven at 350° for about 10 minutes, then let cool.

Layer and repeat the following ingredients in a 9 x 13-inch baking dish:

Spaghetti sauce (I usually use a vodka sauce). Put some on bottom of dish first.

Eggplant slices

Ricotta cheese

Medium onion, finely chopped

Red bell pepper, finely chopped

Fresh baby spinach or kale, generous amount

Prosciutto, sliced into small pieces

Sprinkle some shredded mozzarella cheese and Italian seasoning on top layer before baking.

Cover dish with aluminum foil and bake at 350° for approximately 25-30 minutes.

You can take out the prosciutto and add zucchini and some other vegetables for a meatless option.

JENNIFER LORICH
Devils Tower National Monument

# Calico Beans

1  lb lean ground beef or venison

6  slices bacon, diced

¼  cup onion, chopped

2  cans (approx 16 oz each) baked beans, drained but reserve liquid*

1  can (15 oz) red kidney beans, drained

1  can (15 oz) butter beans, drained

1  can (15 oz) northern beans, drained

¼  cup molasses

½–¾  cup brown sugar

¼  cup ketchup

2  tsp mustard

Brown ground meat with the bacon and onion.

Put all ingredients in slow cooker.

Cover and cook on high for 1 hour.

Reduce to low and cook 3-5 hours.

*Drain the juice in the baked beans and reserve the liquid to use as needed to thin mixture throughout cooking.

LORIEN GRAYSAY
Devils Tower National Monument

# Hamburger Stroganoff

2  T parsley, minced

1  cup sour cream

¼  tsp pepper

1  lb fresh mushrooms

2  T flour

1  lb ground beef

½  cup onion, minced

1  can cream of chicken soup

2  tsp salt

1  clove garlic, minced

1  tsp butter

Lightly brown onion and garlic in butter.

Stir in ground beef and brown.

Stir in flour, salt, pepper and mushrooms, cooking 5 minutes.

Stir in undiluted soup and simmer, uncovered, for about 10 minutes.

Stir in sour cream and heat through.

Sprinkle with parsley.

KIM TAYLOR, ADMINISTRATIVE & ACCOUNTING ASSISTANT
Mount Rushmore Bookstores

# Tzimmes Jeannette (Beef Brisket)

This was a recipe my mother made on special occasions. The dried fruit makes a wonderful sauce for the meat. Sounds kind of weird, but it is delicious.

| | |
|---|---|
| 6–7 | lb boneless beef brisket |
| 2 | T oil |
| 2 | medium onions, sliced |
| ½ | tsp freshly ground pepper |
| ½ | tsp nutmeg |
| 1½ | T brown sugar |
| 1½ | cups water |
| 4 | medium potatoes |
| 8 | carrots, cut in large chunks |
| ¾ | cup dried prunes |
| ¾ | cup dried apricots |

Place meat fat side down in heated Dutch oven or roaster with oil for browning.

Add onion, pepper, nutmeg, brown sugar, and water.

Cover tightly and simmer over low heat or in 300° oven for about 1 ½ hours.

Pare and chunk potatoes and carrots.

Add prunes, apricots, potatoes, and carrots in alternate layers.

Cover and simmer 45 minutes to 1 hour until veggies are tender.

Place the meat, potatoes and carrots on a serving dish.

Serve sauce with prunes, apricots, and onions on the side.

SUE SKROVE
Devils Tower National Monument

# Beer Batter Fried Chicken

| | |
|---|---|
| 12 | pieces of chicken |
| 1 | cup beer |
| | Oil for frying (I mix olive oil and canola oil) |
| 1 | cup all-purpose flour |
| ½ | tsp salt |
| 1½ | tsp parsley, chopped |
| 2 | T onion, finely chopped |

Combine flour and salt in a bowl.

Add in beer until batter is smooth and let it stand about 30 minutes.

Stir in parsley and onions.

Wash the chicken and pat dry.

Sprinkle both sides with salt and pepper.

In a large skillet (I use an electric), heat 2 inches of oil to 350°.

Dip chicken in batter, allowing the excess to drip off.

Carefully place chicken in oil and cook for about 20 minutes, turning occasionally until golden brown. Allow the oil to return to the right temperature before frying each batch.

Remove chicken from the pan and drain on paper towel.

Keep cooked chicken on a baking sheet in preheated 180° oven until all chicken is done.

Be sure to serve right away from the oven.

KIM TAYLOR, ADMINISTRATIVE & ACCOUNTING ASSISTANT
Mount Rushmore Bookstores

# Chalupa

| | | | |
|---|---|---|---|
| 3 | lb pork roast | 1 | tsp oregano |
| 2 | cloves garlic, chopped | 2 | T chili powder |
| 1 | T cumin | 1 | can green peeled chili peppers (not hot) |
| 1 | T salt | 1 | lb pinto beans |

Place all ingredients in large pot and cover with water and lid.

Cook 6 hours.

Take strings off roast and break apart.

Remove cover and cook until thick (doesn't take long).

## SERVE WITH

| | |
|---|---|
| Fritos | Grated cheese |
| Onions, chopped | Avocado, chopped |
| Tomatoes | Ripe olives |
| Lettuce | Salsa or taco sauce |

Place Fritos on plate.

Spread with chalupa and garnish.

Freezes beautifully!

Yield: 8 servings

PAT LEBRUN
Mount Rushmore Society

# Port-a-Pit Chicken

### COMBINE

|       |                    |
|-------|--------------------|
| 6     | cups water         |
| 1⅓    | cups vinegar       |
| 2     | tsps garlic powder |
| ½     | cup brown sugar    |
| ¼     | cup salt           |
| 2     | tsps pepper        |
| 2½    | T Worcestershire   |
| ¾     | stick margarine    |
|       | Pieces of chicken  |

Boil all ingredients together for 15 minutes.

Add pieces of chicken.

Simmer for 20-30 minutes.

Take out chicken and then put it on a grill for another 30 minutes or until done.

PATTY CHILDERS
Badlands National Park

# Husband's Delight (or Quasi-Lasagna)

1½ lb hamburger

8 oz noodles/pasta, cooked and drained

1 can (15 oz) tomato sauce

½ pint sour cream

1 can tomato paste

3 oz cream cheese

1 tsp salt

¾ cup grated cheese (mozzarella/cheddar)

1 tsp garlic powder

1 small onion, chopped

1 tsp sugar

Brown hamburger and drain fat, if necessary.

Add sauce, paste, sugar, salt, garlic powder and onion.

Simmer on low. While simmering sauce, cook noodles (drain) and mix cream cheese with sour cream.

In a casserole dish, layer noodles, meat mixture and cream cheese mixture.

Repeat and then top with grated cheese.

Bake at 300° for 45 minutes.

PATTY CHILDERS
Badlands National Park

# My Kids' Favorite Pizza Casserole

1   lb ground beef (or sausage)

    Garlic salt and pepper to taste

½   pkg pepperoni

1   can pizza sauce

1   pkg (8 oz) egg noodles

2   cups mozzarella cheese

Prepare the egg noodles according to the package directions. Drain.

While noodles are boiling, brown ground beef with garlic salt and pepper to taste.

Add the can of pizza sauce to the beef mixture.

When both are finished cooking, using a small casserole dish, layer the egg noodles, ground beef, pepperoni and top it all off with the mozzarella cheese. May add other toppings such as mushrooms or peppers.

Bake at 375° for 20 minutes. I like to serve with a garden salad and French bread.

ANNA RAUE, EXECUTIVE ADMINISTRATIVE ASSISTANT
Mount Rushmore Society

# Rosemary Chicken Breasts

4  skinless, boneless chicken breast halves

5  garlic cloves, minced

2  T minced fresh rosemary or 1 tsp dried

1  T dijon mustard

1  T lemon juice

¾  tsp salt

½  tsp ground pepper

2  T olive oil

In a small bowl, mix together all ingredients except chicken.

Place chicken breasts in a single layer in glass baking dish.

Pour sauce over chicken and turn to coat well.

Cover and marinate a minimum of ½ hour. Longer for better flavor!

Remove chicken from marinade and place on grill 4-6 inches from heat source.

Grill, turning once and basting once with reserved marinade, until chicken is white throughout but still juicy, about 8-10 minutes.

JODY DAVILA
Wind Cave National Park

# Hoboes

A fun, easy meal that kids can do!

⅓–½ lb hamburger patties for each serving

1 carrot and 1 potato for each serving

Butter, salt and pepper

Cooking spray and foil

Pre-heat oven to 350°.

Tear off a 12-inch piece of foil for each serving.

Spray the foil with cooking spray.

Lay hamburger patty on each piece of foil.

Slice a potato on top of each burger.

Salt and pepper the potato.

Clean a carrot and slice on top of each potato.

Top with a generous dob of butter.

Roll the foil tightly, leaving no gaps.

Bake in oven on a cookie sheet for 1 hour or cook on a grill or over hot coals.

PATTY CHILDERS
Badlands National Park

# Presidential Prime Rib

5 lb ribeye roast

1 cup coarse salt

¼ cup fresh ground pepper

¼ cup garlic powder

¼ cup chopped rosemary

Allow fresh or thawed roast to stand at room temperature for 1 hour.

Rub roast with combined seasonings.

Place on rack in roasting pan with rib side down, fatty side up.

Roast at 400° for 30 minutes.

Turn down to 325° for 1 hour.

Check for desired doneness with meat thermometer.

Let rest for 20 minutes before carving.

DIANA NIELSEN SAATHOFF, EXECUTIVE DIRECTOR
Mount Rushmore Society

# Marinade for Wild Game

1 cup soy sauce

1 cup whiskey

1 cup teriyaki sauce

1 cup Worcestershire sauce

2 tsp lemon pepper seasoning

2–3 whole garlic cloves

Combine ingredients in plastic bag along with pieces of wild game (1–1½-inch pieces work best).

Let marinate for at least 2 hours. Longer is better.

Remove meat and grill until medium rare.

TERRY HUSEBY
Devils Tower Natural History Association

# Stuffed Burger Bundles

1   pkg Stove Top Stuffing, prepared

2   cans cream of mushroom soup

⅓   cup milk

4   tsp Worcestershire sauce

2   lb ground beef

2   T ketchup

Mix milk and ground beef.

Make into patties. I make them large and flat on the counter, about 5 inches in diameter. You can make them smaller, just use less filling.

Put ¼ cup stuffing in the center and seal. Use a 9 x 13-inch cake pan.

Mix the soup, Worcestershire sauce and ketchup and pour over stuffed patties.

Bake at 350° for 1 hour.

ECHO BOHL
Devils Tower Natural History Association

# Mexican Lasagna

| | |
|---|---|
| 1 | pkg corn or flour tortillas |
| 1 | carton (16 oz) cottage cheese |
| 1 | lb ground beef |
| 1 | cup salsa |
| 1 | egg |
| 1 | can (15 oz) tomato sauce |
| 1 | tsp oregano |
| 1 | pkg taco seasoning mix |
| 1½ | cups shredded cheese |

Brown meat and drain.

Stir in salsa, sauce and taco seasoning. Simmer 5 minutes.

Combine cottage cheese, egg and oregano.

Spray 9 x 13-inch pan with cooking spray.

Line with tortillas, overlapping the edges.

Layer ½ of the meat mixture, spoon cottage cheese mixture over the meat and then add another layer of tortillas.

Top with remaining meat mixture and shredded cheese.

Bake at 375° for 30-35 minutes or until bubbly.

*Can also add a layer of beans if desired

PATTY CHILDERS
Badlands National Park

# Spicy Pulled Pork

This makes a great party sandwich or use it for tacos or quesadillas.

2   onions, peeled and quartered

1   pork shoulder roast

    Salt and pepper to taste

2   cans (12 oz) Dr. Pepper

4   T packed brown sugar

½   cup chipotle chiles in adobo sauce (less if you like it milder)

Place in a crockpot on low and cook for 6-8 hours until fork tender.

Spoon off any fat on top and keep it in the broth while serving.

DIANA NIELSEN SAATHOFF, EXECUTIVE DIRECTOR
Mount Rushmore Society

# Aunt Annie's Chicken Marinade

This makes enough for 6 chicken breasts.

| | | |
|---|---|---|
| ½ | cup brown sugar | |
| ⅓ | cup olive oil | |
| ¼ | cup vinegar | |
| 3 | cloves garlic, crushed | |
| 3 | T yellow mustard | |
| 1½ | T lemon juice | |
| 1½ | T lime juice | |
| 1½ | tsp salt | |
| ¼ | tsp pepper | |

Mix all ingredients.

Add chicken and marinate 12-24 hours.

Grill or bake as desired.

PATTY CHILDERS
Badlands National Park

# *Side Dishes*

## DEVILS TOWER NATIONAL MONUMENT

This geologic feature protrudes 1,267 feet out of the rolling prairie that surrounds the Black Hills in Wyoming. The site is considered sacred to the Lakota and other tribes who have a connection with the area. Hundreds of parallel cracks make it one of the finest traditional crack-climbing areas in North America.

LOCATED NEAR HULETT, WY
Supported by Devils Tower Natural History Association

*"There are things in nature that engender an awful quiet in the heart of man: Devils Tower is one of them."*—N. Scott Momaday, The Way to Rainy Mountain

**Falcons fly high above Devils Tower.**

# Stuffed Sweet Potatoes

One of President Calvin Coolidge's favorites and served at a Mount Rushmore dinner in 2007.

6 medium sweet potatoes or yams, scrubbed and rubbed well with oil.

Pierce with fork and bake at 400° until soft (about 1 hour).

Let cool slightly.

Slice in half and scoop out the potato.

Mash the potato until smooth.

BLEND IN

1 can (8½ oz) crushed pineapple, drained

1 can (6 oz) frozen orange juice concentrate, thawed

¼ tsp salt

½ cup walnuts, chopped (optional)

Stuff potato shells with the mixture.

Refrigerate covered for several hours or overnight.

Heat oven to 400° and bake uncovered for 30 minutes.

Sprinkle with 1 cup miniature marshmallows.

Continue baking until melted, about 5-7 minutes.

Yield: 12 servings

# Delmonico Potatoes

One of Abraham Lincoln's favorites and served at a Mount Rushmore dinner in 2006.

| | |
|---|---|
| 4 medium white potatoes | ¼ tsp white pepper |
| ¾ cup whole milk | ¼ tsp nutmeg, grated |
| ¼ cup heavy whipping cream | 2 T Parmesan cheese, grated |
| ½ tsp salt | |

Wash (but do not skin) the potatoes and quarter them lengthwise (so that, after cooking, they can be grated into the longest shreds possible).

Bring 8 cups of water to a boil and then add the potatoes.

Let boil for 10 minutes so that the potatoes are not cooked through.

Immediately submerse the hot potatoes into cold water and let them cool for at least 30 minutes.

Grate the potatoes into long strips.

Mix together in a bowl the milk, cream, salt, pepper and nutmeg.

Preheat a large frying pan over medium heat and then add the potatoes and liquid mixture.

Fold them together well but gently, without mashing the potatoes, and cook for 10 minutes, mixing lightly occasionally so that they do not burn.

Remove from the stove and fold in 1 T of the cheese.

Transfer the potatoes into a pre-buttered baking dish and arrange evenly.

On top, sprinkle the remaining 1 T of cheese.

Preheat the oven to 425°.

Place the uncovered baking dish into the upper third of the oven.

Bake for 6 minutes or until lightly browned.

Yield: 4-6 servings

Serve immediately.

# Spicy Wild Rice

2 cups stock or water

1 cup uncooked wild rice

½ tsp (or more depending on taste) Cayenne Seasoning

8 oz fresh or dried mushrooms

1 T butter or olive oil

1 cup celery, diced

1 can cream of mushroom soup

Salt and pepper to taste

## OPTIONAL

Any nuts – almonds, pecans, hazelnuts

You can also substitute other vegetables such as broccoli or squash

Combine the rice, liquid and seasoning in a 2-quart saucepan.

Cook at a low temp until the rice kernels pop open and all liquid is absorbed (at least 2 hours).

While rice is cooking, sauté mushrooms in butter/olive oil to desired doneness. I like them to have a little crust on them.

Add celery and continue to sauté until celery is al dente.

Combine mushroom/celery mixture and soup with rice. If too thick, add a little milk.

Season with salt and pepper.

Can be served hot or cold.

## PATTY RESSLER, EXECUTIVE DIRECTOR
Black Hills Parks & Forests Association

# Crock Pot Stuffing

| | | | | |
|---|---|---|---|---|
| 1 | cup butter | ½ | tsp marjoram |
| 2 | cups onion, diced | 1 | tsp poultry seasoning |
| 2 | cups celery, diced | 2 | cans (8 oz) mushrooms, drained |
| ¼ | cup parsley, chopped | 15–16 | cups slightly dried bread cubes |
| 1 | tsp salt | 4 | cups turkey or chicken broth |
| ½ | tsp pepper | 2 | eggs, beaten |
| 1 | tsp sage | | Cooked giblets (optional) |
| 1 | tsp thyme | | |

Melt butter in skillet and sauté onions, celery, mushrooms and parsley.

Pour over bread crumbs in large bowl.

Add seasonings to broth and eggs and pour over bread mixture.

Pack lightly in large crock pot and cook on high for 45 minutes.

Turn down to low and cook for 4-8 hours.

Check periodically to see if it is too dry.

This is an excellent alternative to stuffing a turkey, and it's delicious!

BETTY ERICKSON KORZAN
Kimball, SD

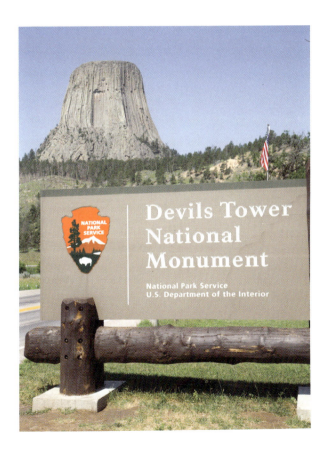

# Kris' Green Tomato Casserole

This is a yummy way to use up green tomatoes at season's end.

Layer sliced green tomatoes with grated cheddar cheese, about 3 or 4 layers.

End with cheese, salt, and pepper and a few dabs of butter.

Bake at 350˚ for about 30 minutes or longer.

If you put the green tomatoes in the fridge, they will not ripen and will keep for 3 weeks or so.

KRIS SEARS
Reno, NV


# Rice Pilaf

| | |
|---|---|
| 1 | can Campbell's beef consommé or beef broth |
| 1 | can Campbell's French onion soup |
| 2 | cans sliced mushrooms, undrained |
| 1 | cup rice, uncooked |
| ½ | stick butter |

Melt butter.

Pour in rest of ingredients. No need to mix.

Bake at 400˚ for 30 minutes or in microwave on high 25 minutes (depending on wattage). Basically, bake until there is no liquid.

Yield: 6 servings

*"I love the national parks because they are just untouched beauty."*

DEBBIE MONDILLO
Easton, PA

# Grilled Salmon Marinade

4-6   wild salmon fillets, fresh

MARINATE IN

2   T raspberry vinegar

2   T sugar

2   tsp grill seasoning

Marinate for 2 hours or longer.

Grill 3-4 minutes each side or to desired doneness. May also broil.

I like to use a non-stick aluminum foil on the grill to make it easy to turn the delicate salmon.

DIANA NIELSEN SAATHOFF, EXECUTIVE DIRECTOR
Mount Rushmore Society

# Asiago Cheese Soufflés

1 cup Asiago cheese, grated

8 eggs

1 cup half & half

Lemon pepper salt

Preheat oven to 375°.

Prepare 4 (7 oz) ramekins by spraying with Pam.

Place ramekins in a 9 x 13-inch baking pan.

In a measuring cup, break 2 eggs and whip until frothy.

Add 1 T grated cheese and a dash of lemon pepper salt.

Pour enough half & half into measuring cup to bring mixture to ¾ cups.

Pour mixture into prepared ramekin.

Repeat for each of the 4 ramekins.

Place baking pan with ramekins into oven and bake at 375° for 25 minutes.

Sprinkle remaining cheese on top of soufflés and bake 5 more minutes.

Serve immediately.

Yield: 4 servings

**EILEEN ROSSOW & WARREN MEYER**
Mount Rushmore Society

# Chantilly Potatoes

4   cups potatoes, mashed

¼   cup butter

1½   tsp salt

   Pepper

3   cans (12 oz) French fried onions

1   cup cream, whipped

⅔   cup cheddar cheese, shredded

1½   T parsley

Combine butter, potatoes, salt and pepper and mix well.

Stir in 2 cans onions.

Spoon into greased 1½-quart casserole.

Combine whipped cream, cheese, salt and blend well.

Spread over potatoes.

Sprinkle with parsley.

Bake 325° for 25-30 minutes.

Top with 1 can onions.

JUDY DUHAMEL
Mount Rushmore Society

# Pineapple Casserole

This recipe showed up at a National Park Service potluck. Like bread pudding, it is a great side for ham or pork. It is very good and is very easy to make.

½   lb butter

5   slices white bread, torn up

2   eggs, beaten

1   T flour

½   tsp salt

½   cup sugar

1   #2 can crushed pineapple with juice (about 2½ cups)

Add beaten eggs to pineapple and mix.

Add other ingredients.

Bake at 375° for 1 hour.

MEG WEHRSTEDT
Klondike Gold Rush National Historical Park

# Yakitori Sauce

This is delicious as well as beautiful. Other vegetables can be used, and I think chicken or beef could also be good marinated in the sauce.

1   T peanut oil

½   cup soy sauce

2   T dry white sherry

1   T sesame seeds

1   T sugar

Combine all ingredients in saucepan and bring to a boil.

Cook for about 4 minutes or until the liquid thickens. Let cool.

1   green pepper

1   red pepper

1   yellow pepper

1   orange pepper

1   sweet onion

Mushrooms

Cut vegetables into ½- to 1-inch pieces.

Marinate in yakitori sauce for an hour.

Put in grill basket and cook on hot grill 12-15 minutes.

PAT LEBRUN
Mount Rushmore Society

# *Desserts*

## CUSTER STATE PARK

With 71,000 acres, Custer State Park is one of the largest, most distinctive state parks in the nation and is home to a herd of 1,300 bison. Lakes, natural areas and hiking are abundant, including Harney Peak, which is the tallest peak in South Dakota.

LOCATED NEAR CUSTER, SD
Supported by Black Hills Parks & Forests Association

Regarding driving through Custer State Park via the Needles Highway and Iron Mountain Road:

*"You're not supposed to drive here at 60 miles an hour. To do the scenery half justice, people should drive at 20 or under; to do it full justice, they should get out and walk."—Senator Peter Norbeck*

# FDR's Birthday Cake

One of President Franklin Delano Roosevelt's favorites and served at a Mount Rushmore dinner in 2008.

| | |
|---|---|
| 1 | cup butter or margarine |
| 1½ | cups sugar |
| 3 | eggs, well beaten |
| 1 | cup cold black coffee |
| 2 | cups flour |
| ½ | cup cocoa powder |
| ½ | tsp salt |
| ½ | tsp vanilla extract |
| 1 | tsp baking soda |
| 1 | T vinegar |

Cream butter and add sugar, a little at a time. Cream well.

Add beaten eggs.

Sift flour, salt, soda and cocoa together 3 times.

Add dry ingredients to batter.

Add vinegar and vanilla.

Bake at 350° in 9-inch layer pan for 20-35 minutes or in loaf pan for 30-40 minutes.

# William Howard Taft's Pumpkin Pie

Adapted from the Capitol Hill Cookbook. One of President William H. Taft's favorites and served at a Mount Rushmore dinner in 2013.

|  |  |
|---|---|
| 1 | homemade or purchased 9-inch pie crust |
| ¼ | cup sugar |
| ½ | cup brown sugar |
| ½ | tsp salt |
| ¼ | tsp allspice |
| 1 | tsp cinnamon |
| ½ | tsp ginger |
| 1½ | cups pumpkin, canned or cooked |
| 2 | eggs, separated |
| ¾ | cup canned evaporated milk |
| ¾ | cup whole milk |

Mix sugars, salt and spices.

Add pumpkin.

Add egg yolks and all milk.

Beat egg whites until just stiff and fold into pumpkin mixture.

Pour into pie shell.

Bake at 450° for 10 minutes, then turn down temperature to 350° and bake 30-40 minutes until knife comes out of filling clean.

Serve with ice cream or whipped cream.

# Zucchini Cake

This freezes well. If you want to make 2 loaves of zucchini bread, just increase flour to 3 cups.

|   |   |
|---|---|
| 3 | eggs, beaten |
| 2 | cups sugar |
| 1 | cup oil |
| 2 | cups zucchini, grated |
| 2 | cups flour |
| 1 | tsp baking soda |
| 2-3 | tsp cinnamon |
| 1 | tsp salt |
| ¼ | tsp baking powder |
| 1 | cup nuts or raisins (optional) |

Mix and pour into greased, floured 9 x 13-inch pan.

Bake at 325° for 1 hour or until set.

GLAZE

|   |   |
|---|---|
| ½ | cup evaporated milk |
| 1 | cup sugar |
| ¾ | stick butter |
| 1 | tsp vanilla |

Boil until thickened.

Make holes in the cake with a fork and pour over while still warm.

RUTH SAMUELSEN
Mount Rushmore Society

# Oreo Cookie Ice Cream Dessert

24  Oreo chocolate sandwich cookies, crushed

2  T butter, melted

½  gallon any kind of ice cream, such as chocolate and vanilla ripple, mint (green) with chocolate bits or any chocolate combination

Cool Whip and Hershey's Chocolate Syrup

Combine Oreos and butter and press into 9 x 13-inch pan.

Then, slice ice cream.

Place ice cream slices on cookie crust and spread the top lightly to hide the cracks.

Drizzle Hershey's Chocolate Syrup over top.

Spread Cool Whip on top.

Freeze.

DIANE KORZAN WELLER
Mitchell, SD

# Honey Cake

2½  cups all-purpose flour

1  cup sugar

1  cup honey

1  cup sour cream

2  eggs

2  T vegetable oil

1  tsp baking soda

1½  tsp pumpkin pie spice

Mix dry ingredients separately from the wet ingredients and then blend all together.

Place in two 8½ x 4½ x 2½-inch loaf pans lined with parchment paper. Note: Do not fill to rim. Leave about 1-inch at top of pan.

Bake at 350˚ for 45-55 minutes. Check for doneness with bamboo testing sticks. If the sticks come out dry, the honey cakes are done.

Cool on racks.

BRUCE WEISMAN, CHIEF OF NATURAL RESOURCES
Mount Rushmore National Memorial

# Buckeyes

I got this recipe while attending a meeting in Cincinnati. Supposedly, it is Ohio's official state cookie.

## CREAM TOGETHER

- 2 sticks butter or margarine
- 2 cups peanut butter
- 2 tsp vanilla
- 5 cups powdered sugar

Shape into 1-inch balls.

Refrigerate until they set up.

## MELT IN DOUBLE BOILER

- 12 oz chocolate chips
- ¼ bar paraffin or professional dipping chocolate

Using toothpicks, dip chilled balls into chocolate until mostly covered, leaving the top uncovered to give appearance of a buckeye.

EILEEN DIXON FLEISHACKER
Mount Rushmore Society

# Our Favorite Chocolate Chip Cookies

To make these cookies, cool the dough before baking and remember to always use butter in them.

      1  cup butter, softened

      1  cup white sugar

      1  cup brown sugar

      2  eggs

   2–3  tsp vanilla

      3  cups flour

      1  tsp soda

     ½  tsp salt

   2–3  cups chocolate chips

      1  cup pecans or walnuts

Cream butter and sugars.

Add eggs and vanilla.

Stir in the flour, soda and salt.

Add chocolate chips and pecans and mix.

Cool the dough for awhile in the refrigerator before baking.

Then roll into balls and place on a cookie sheet.

Bake at 350° until lightly browned on the edges, about 8-10 minutes.

KAREN POPPE
Wall, SD

# Lois Apple Crisp

4 cups apples, peeled and sliced (about 8 medium apples or 4 large Granny Smith apples)

Mound in a buttered pie pan.

Sprinkle with ¼ cup orange juice.

## IN A BOWL, MIX

1 cup sugar

¾ cup flour

½ tsp cinnamon

¼ tsp nutmeg

Dash of salt

Cut in ½ cup butter or margarine.

Pat on top of the apple mound.

Bake at 375° for 45 minutes.

RUTH SAMUELSEN
Mount Rushmore Society

# Mamie Eisenhower's Million Dollar Fudge

One of President Dwight D. Eisenhower's favorites and served at a Mount Rushmore dinner in 2010.

4½ cups sugar

Pinch of salt

2 T butter

1 tall can evaporated milk

12 oz semi-sweet chocolate bits

12 oz German's sweet chocolate

1 pint marshmallow cream

2 cups nutmeats

Boil the sugar, salt, butter, evaporated milk together for 6 minutes.

Put chocolate bits, German's chocolate, marshmallow cream and nutmeats in a bowl.

Pour the boiling syrup over the ingredients.

Beat until chocolate is melted, then pour in pan.

Let stand a few hours before cutting.

Remember, it is better the second day.

Store in tin box.

# Hunter's Cookies

## CREAM TOGETHER

2 cups shortening

2 cups brown sugar

1 cup white sugar

## ADD

2 tsp vanilla

2 tsp baking soda

1 tsp salt

## PUSH TO ONE SIDE AND ADD

5 eggs, beaten

5 cups flour

Stir in a 12 oz package of chocolate chips.

May add dates, raisins or nuts in addition to (or instead of) chocolate chips.

Drop on slightly greased cookie sheets and bake at 350° for 10-12 minutes.

Yield: 6-7 dozen

EILEEN DIXON FLEISHACKER
Mount Rushmore Society

# Kathleen's Cranberry Pie

2 cups fresh cranberries

½ cup sugar

½ cup chopped nuts

Mix and place in well-greased pie pan.

2 eggs

1 cup sugar

1 cup flour

½ cup butter, melted

Beat and pour over cranberries

Bake at 325° for 1 hour.

Serve with whipped cream.

KATHLEEN MEYER
Fort Collins, CO

# Badlands Batter Cheesecake

## BATTER

| | |
|---|---|
| 1 cup sugar | 2 cups flour |
| ½ tsp salt | 2 eggs |
| 1 cup butter | 2 tsp baking powder |

## CHEESE FILLING

| | |
|---|---|
| 2 pkgs (8 oz) cream cheese | ½ cup sugar |
| 1 egg, beaten | 1 tsp vanilla |

Blend sugar and vanilla together and then mix with cream cheese and egg.

## STREUSEL TOPPING

| | |
|---|---|
| ¼ cup sugar | 2 T butter |
| ¼ cup flour | |

Mix to coarse crumb texture.

For batter, cream butter and sugar.

Add eggs and beat well.

Add dry ingredients.

Spread ⅔ of batter into flat bottom of spring-form pan.

Spread cheese mixture evenly over batter.

Spoon remaining batter on top of cheese mixture spaced out in dollops.

Sprinkle with streusel.

Bake at 350˚ for 45 minutes. Cool completely before serving.

*"I love national parks because you get to experience some of the most beautiful places in the country in the purest and most unrestricted way."*

ANN HENRICHSEN
Badlands Natural History Association

# Christmas Cranberry Cake

| | |
|---|---|
| 2   small eggs | 4½  T butter |
| 1½  cups sugar | 1   tsp vanilla |
| 3   cups cake flour | ¾   cup walnuts |
| 1½  cups milk | 3   cups whole raw cranberries |
| 1   T baking powder | ½   tsp salt |

Beat eggs, sugar, butter, and vanilla together.

Add dry ingredients alternately with milk.

Fold in cranberries and nuts and pour into greased 9 x 13-inch pan.

Bake at 350° for 35 minutes.

SERVE WARM WITH HOT SAUCE AS FOLLOWS

| | |
|---|---|
| ½   cup butter | ½   cup brown sugar |
| ½   cup cream | 1   tsp vanilla or 1 T rum |
| ½   cup white sugar | |

Bring the first four ingredients to a boil and add vanilla or rum.

Beat and serve over cake.

(For an extra-festive mood, place a sugar cube that has been soaked briefly in lemon extract on top of each piece of cake and light with a match just before serving.)

COOK'S NOTE: The cake and the sauce freeze well. In fact, the sauce is better when reheated.

JODY KETEL
Mount Rushmore Society

# Orange-Chocolate Meltaways

  1  pkg milk chocolate chips

  1  cup semi-sweet chocolate chips

  ¾  cup whipping cream

  1  tsp grated orange peel

  2½  tsp orange extract

## COATING

  1  cup milk chocolate chips

  2  T shortening

Place chocolate chips in mixing bowl and set aside.

In a saucepan, bring cream and orange peel to a gentle boil.

Immediately pour over chips.

Let stand 1 minute and whisk until smooth.

Add the extract and stir.

Cover and chill for 35 minutes or until the mixture begins to thicken.

Beat for 10-15 seconds or just until mixture lightens in color. DO NOT OVERBEAT.

Spoon rounded teaspoons onto waxed paper-lined sheet. (You can roll perfectly shaped balls by hand but you must work quickly.)

Cover and chill 5 minutes.

In microwave, melt chocolate and shortening for the coating and stir until smooth.

Dip balls in the coating and place on waxed paper to harden.

Store in refrigerator.

DAWN MILLER
Garretson, SD

# St. Nicholas "Sinterklas" Cookies

8 cups flour

3 cups butter

3 cups brown sugar

3 eggs

1 tsp baking powder

4 tsp cinnamon

2 tsp cloves, ground

Mix and knead like bread dough.

Roll in loaves (about 2 x 4 inches) and let stand all night in a cool place.

Slice thin (about ⅓-inch thick).

Bake at 350° for about 10-12 minutes until brown around edges.

Let sit on cookie sheet for 1 minute to firm before removing to cooling rack.

MAX PESCHEL & GIAN MERCURIO
Mesa Verde National Park

# Cherry Dessert (Our Favorite February Dessert)

|       |                              |
|-------|------------------------------|
| 1½    | cups crushed vanilla wafers  |
| 4     | T melted butter              |

Combine and press into 9 x 13-inch pan.

|       |                                                              |
|-------|--------------------------------------------------------------|
| 1     | can sweetened condensed milk                                 |
| ⅓–½   | cup fresh lemon juice (2 lemons)                             |
| 1     | can tart red pitted cherries, drained (add last if adding food coloring) |
| 1     | cup chopped pecans                                           |
| 3     | cups Cool Whip                                              |

Combine sweetened condensed milk and lemon juice.

Fold in Cool Whip, pecans and cherries. (I add 2 drops of red food coloring to give it a pink color.)

Spread over crumb crust. Chill and serve with Cool Whip and more nuts if desired.

JODY KETEL
Mount Rushmore Society

# Chocolate Sheet Cake

This cake has shown up at many National Park Service potlucks over the years. I don't usually do a lot of scratch baking, but this cake is worth the effort if you have chocolate lovers around.

| | |
|---|---|
| 2 cups sugar, sifted | 1 cup water |
| 2 cups flour | 2 eggs, slightly beaten |
| 1 stick Parkay margarine | ½ cup buttermilk or sour milk |
| 1 cup cooking oil | 1 tsp baking soda |
| 4 T cocoa powder | 1 tsp vanilla |

Sift flour and sugar together in big bowl and set aside.

Bring margarine, cooking oil, cocoa powder and water to boil and pour over dry ingredients. Mix.

Add eggs, buttermilk or sour milk, soda and vanilla. Mix.

Pour into floured sheet cake pan and bake at 400° for 25 minutes or until it springs back when pressed.

## ICING

| | |
|---|---|
| 1 stick Parkay margarine | 1 box (1 lb) powdered sugar |
| 4 T cocoa powder | ½ tsp vanilla |
| 6 T milk | 1 cup chopped nuts |

Bring margarine, cocoa powder and milk just to boil. Do not scorch.

Add powdered sugar and vanilla. Sprinkle chopped nuts on top. Spread frosting on warm cake.

MONA WAUGH
Hulett, WY

# Fudge – The Best Ever

This fudge recipe has been something of a "valley secret" since the 1940s. The valley runs for about 8 miles along Highway 36 from Mount Rushmore's east entrance nearly to Highway 79. Gutzon Borglum's place is in the valley, just east of the Lintz Ranch, where my grandma still lives. Her name is Elouise Lintz, and she's 91 years old.

## IN A LARGE MIXING BOWL, MIX

2 cups mini marshmallows

1½ cups semi-sweet chocolate chips

1 tsp vanilla

## IN A SAUCEPAN, COMBINE

⅔ cup evaporated milk

Pinch of salt

2 T butter

1½ cups sugar

Butter a 9 x 9-inch cake pan; set aside.

Bring mixture in saucepan to a roiling boil, stirring constantly for 6 minutes or until the surface of the mixture is shiny.

Pour hot mixture into mixing bowl.

Stir vigorously until chocolate and marshmallows are completely melted and the mixture is smooth.

Pour contents of mixing bowl into buttered cake pan and let cool.

MARNIE HERRMANN
Mount Rushmore Society

# Fudge Truffle Cheesecake

FOR CHOCOLATE CRUMB CRUST, COMBINE IN MEDIUM BOWL

1½  cups vanilla wafer crumbs

½  cup powdered sugar

⅓  cup Hershey's cocoa powder

⅓  cup melted butter

Press firmly on bottom of 9-inch spring form pan.

2  cups Hershey's semi-sweet chocolate chips

3  pkgs (8 oz) cream cheese, room temperature

1  can (14 oz) sweetened condensed milk

4  eggs

2  tsp vanilla

Heat oven to 300°.

In heavy saucepan, over very low heat, melt chips, stirring constantly.

In large mixer bowl, beat cheese until fluffy.

Gradually beat in sweetened condensed milk until smooth.

Add melted chips and remaining ingredients and mix well. Pour into prepared pan.

Bake 65 minutes or until center is set.

Cool and chill.

SUE SKROVE
Devils Tower National Monument

# Buttermilk Brownies

2 cups sugar

2 cups flour

4 T cocoa powder

½ cup buttermilk

2 eggs

1 tsp baking soda

1 cup water

1 stick butter

½ cup oil

Sift sugar, flour, baking soda and cocoa together in bowl.

Combine water, butter and oil in a saucepan and bring to a boil.

Pour over dry ingredients and beat until creamy.

Add eggs and buttermilk. Beat thoroughly.

Bake in greased jelly roll pan for 18 minutes at 400°.

While baking, mix together the following ingredients. Frost while warm.

## FROSTING

½ cup butter

¼ cup cocoa powder

⅓ cup buttermilk

1 box powdered sugar

½ tsp vanilla

Bring butter, cocoa and buttermilk to a boil in small saucepan.

Add powdered sugar and vanilla.

Spread over warm brownies.

AMY KLEIN-GREBA
Devils Tower, WY

# Pastel Cookies

¾  cup shortening

1  tsp vanilla

½  cup sugar

2½  cups flour

1  pkg (3 oz) fruit Jello

1  tsp baking powder

2  eggs

1  tsp salt

Mix shortening, sugar, Jello, eggs and vanilla.

Blend in dry ingredients.

Roll into ¾-inch balls and roll in sugar.

Place on ungreased cookie sheet 3 inches apart.

Flatten with a glass.

Bake at 400° for 6-8 minutes.

Yield: 4 dozen

ECHO BOHL
Devils Tower Natural History Association

# Swedish Rice Pudding

This recipe is from Iris Lange and was handed down from her Swedish Grandmother Aronson.

⅓ cup rice, boiled for 10 minutes and drained

## ADD THE FOLLOWING INGREDIENTS TO DRAINED RICE AND BOIL FOR 5 MINUTES

| | |
|---|---|
| 2 cups milk | Pinch of salt |
| 2 T sugar | 1 tsp butter |

## IN BAKING DISH, MIX

| | |
|---|---|
| 4 eggs, beaten | 2 cups milk |
| ½ cup sugar | 1 tsp vanilla |
| ½ tsp nutmeg (optional) | Cinnamon to taste |

Stir rice mixture into egg mixture.

Sprinkle cinnamon on top and bake over water in 350° oven until done, about 1 ½ hours.

ARDIE BARBER
Mount Rushmore Society

# Sticky Date Pudding

.1  pkg (1 cup) pitted dates

1¼  cups water

1  tsp baking soda

¾  cup caster sugar

2  oz butter

2  eggs

1  cup self-rising flour, sifted


SAUCE

1  cup brown sugar

1  cup cream

2  oz butter

Combine dates and water in saucepan and bring to boil.

Remove from heat, add baking soda and stand 5 mins.

Blend till smooth.

In separate bowl, cream butter and sugar together. Add eggs one at a time.

Gently fold in sifted flour and then date mixture.

Pour into 9-inch cake tin and bake for 55 minutes at 350°.

Check cake and if turning dark, cover with foil until center sets.

Let stand for 10 minutes before putting on rack.

Combine all sauce ingredients and simmer for 3 minutes. Don't boil. Stir while heating.

Pour ¼ cup sauce over cake and put it back in the oven, uncovered, for 10 minutes.

LORRAINE RABBITS
New South Wales, Australia

# Banaffee Pie

This is a fun, quick pie that is perfect any time of year.

| | |
|---|---|
| 1 | graham cracker crust |
| 1 | can Dulce de Leche Caramel (carmelized sweetened condensed milk. Find it in the Hispanic foods section) |
| 3-4 | ripe bananas |
| 1½ | cups heavy cream or whipping cream |
| ½ | cup dark chocolate shavings or dark chocolate chips |

Slice bananas into the pie crust.

Drop the caramel by small spoonfuls over the bananas. The caramel is very thick but will settle in between the banana slices.

In a separate bowl, whip the heavy cream until light and fluffy. Do not add sugar to the whipped cream, as the caramel is very sweet and the unsweetened whipping cream creates a nice balance.

Spread over the caramel layer.

Shave dark chocolate over the top of the pie.

Chill and serve.

LORRAINE RABBITS
New South Wales, Australia

# Strawberry Pie (A Big-Time Favorite)

This was the recipe of Nellie Bottum, wife of former South Dakota Senator Joe Bottum. She had a beautiful yard. When I was a child, my mother and I would often enjoy her backyard in the summer with iced tea or lemonade and her famous strawberry pie.

1   baked pie shell

1   pkg (8 oz) Philadelphia cream cheese

    Whipping cream

1   qt strawberries

Add a little of the whipping cream to cream cheese to make smooth and spread on the bottom of pie shell.

Stick some berries with points up in the cream cheese.

Take rest of berries, mash and cook with about 1 cup sugar and 1 T flour.

Cook on stovestop slowly, about 15 minutes. Let cool.

Pour over strawberries in pie shell and cool about 6 hours.

Top with whipped cream and garnish with whole berries.

COOK'S NOTE: I sometimes cook berries the night before and refrigerate just to make it easier.

JUDY DUHAMEL
Mount Rushmore Society

# German Chocolate Cake Frosting

1 cup sugar

4 egg yolks

1 cup evaporated milk

½ cup butter

1 tsp vanilla

10 oz grated or frozen coconut

1½ cups pecans (or walnuts), chopped

Combine sugar, yolks and evaporated milk in saucepan, preferably in a double boiler.

Stir with whisk until yolks are incorporated.

Add the butter.

Bring to low boil and simmer for 12–15 minutes longer, stirring constantly until it thickens.

Remove from stove and add nuts, vanilla and coconut. Cool.

Spread over your favorite chocolate cake and share.

DAVID BOLTON
Spring Hill, Kansas

# Moses 7-Layer Bars

This was my dad's favorite dessert that my mom made growing up. I still love them, and they are so easy to make.

| | | |
|---|---|---|
| 1 | stick butter | |
| 2 | cups graham cracker crumbs | |
| 1 | cup chocolate chips | |
| 1 | cup butterscotch chips | |
| 1 | cup walnut pieces | |
| 1 | cup coconut, shredded | |
| 1 | can sweetened condensed milk | |

Melt butter in the bottom of a 9 x 9-inch pan.

Pat graham cracker crumbs into butter.

Layer chocolate chips, butterscotch chips, walnuts and coconut, in that order.

Pour condensed milk over, covering ingredients.

Bake 350° for 25 minutes or until light brown on top.

*"My two favorite national parks are Grand Canyon National Park and Mount Rushmore National Memorial. I love the Grand Canyon because of its awe-inspiring beauty, and I love Mount Rushmore because it represents the perseverance of the human spirit in carving a mountain."*

DEBBIE MOSES KETEL, COMMUNICATIONS DIRECTOR
Mount Rushmore Society

AUTHORIZED
PERSONNEL
ONLY

# Beverages

"Americans enjoy a really wonderful gift, and sometimes I don't think they realize the gift is theirs—that is of our national parks. It's up to each of us as individuals to take care of those parks, to love those parks and to become stewards of those parks. I believe the more we get out and enjoy these special places set aside for us, the more meaningful they become for the next generation."

DIANA NIELSEN SAATHOFF, EXECUTIVE DIRECTOR
Mount Rushmore Society

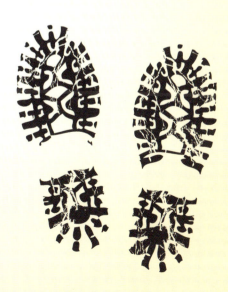

# Russian Tea

¾ cup instant tea powder

2 cups Tang powder

¾ cup lemonade powder

1 cup sugar

1½ tsp cinnamon

¾ tsp cloves

Combine all ingredients into a large plastic or glass container with a tight-fitting lid and shake to mix. Use 2–3 heaping spoonfuls per large glass or mug.

Fill with boiling water.

Stir well with spoon and enjoy after it cools slightly.

JODY KETEL
Mount Rushmore Society

# Spicy Perk-a-Punch

This punch adds a festive aroma to your home during the holidays.

- 2 qt cranberry juice
- 2 qt unsweetened pineapple juice
- 1 qt water
- 1 T whole cloves
- 1 T whole allspice
- 4 2-inch cinnamon sticks
- ⅔ cup brown sugar
- 2 lemons, washed and quartered

Pour first 3 ingredients into bottom of a large electric percolator.

In top basket, place next 5 ingredients and perk until done

Juice will perk up through the basket, blending all of the ingredients.

JODY KETEL
Mount Rushmore Society

# Submitter Index

The following people submitted the recipes featured in this cookbook. We thank them for their support of our treasured parks.

# Recipe Index

## Entrées

Momma Millie's Biftek Miramonde 70

Pepper & Ginger BBQ Ribs 71

Hamburger Goulash 72

Linda's Party Sandwiches 73

Chicken Breasts Diane 74

Colorado Chicken 75

Never-Fail Cheesy Rice Casserole 76

Pasta with Sausage and Broccoli 77

Cilantro Lime Chicken 78

Crusted Cheddar Chicken Breasts 79

Bucky's Chili 80

Berdell's Meat Loaf 81

Gramma Sis' Savory Spaghetti Sauce 82

Hot Beef Sammies 83

Susan's Hot Chick(en) Dish 84

Prime Steak Rub 85

Baked Trout with Parsley Stuffing 86

Salmon on a Cedar Plank 87

Herbed Pork Roast 88

Eggplant Casserole 89

Calico Beans 90

Hamburger Stroganoff 91

Tzimmes Jeannette (Beef Brisket) 92

Beer Batter Fried Chicken 93

Chalupa 94

Port-a-Pit Chicken 95

Husband's Delight (or Quasi-Lasagna) 96

My Kids' Favorite Pizza Casserole 97

Rosemary Chicken Breasts 98

Hoboes 99

Presidential Prime Rib 100

Marinade for Wild Game 101

Stuffed Burger Bundles 102

Mexican Lasagna 103

Spicy Pulled Pork 104

Aunt Annie's Chicken Marinade 105

## Side Dishes

Stuffed Sweet Potatoes 108

Delmonico Potatoes 109

Spicy Wild Rice 110

Crock Pot Stuffing 111

Kris' Green Tomato Casserole 112

Rice Pilaf 112

Grilled Salmon Marinade 113

Asiago Cheese Souffles 114

Chantilly Potatoes 115

Pineapple Casserole 116

Yakitori Sauce 117

## Desserts

FDR's Birthday Cake 120

William Howard Taft's Pumpkin Pie 121

Zucchini Cake 122

Oreo Cookie Ice Cream Dessert 123

Honey Cake 124

Buckeyes 125

## *Beverages*

# Photo Credits

Photos provided by Shutterstock unless otherwise noted below.

p. 4: Chad Coppess

p. 6: (l-r) NPS, NPS, NPS, Rodger Slott; NPS; BethAnn Herman; BethAnn Herman

p. 7: Chad Coppess

p. 8: NPS

p. 13: NPS

p. 14: Chad Coppess

p. 19: Debi White

p. 23: Cheryl A. Schreier

p. 25: Chad Coppess

p. 26: BethAnn Herman

p. 35: Ruth Samuelsen

p. 38: Debbie Moses Ketel

p. 49: NPS

p. 60: top NPS; bottom left BethAnn Herman

p. 62: Chad Coppess

p. 63: top BethAnn Herman

p. 64: top Rise Photo; bottom right Lincoln Borglum Collection

p. 66: left Chad Coppess; middle NPS; bottom right Kathy McClelland

p. 67: top, middle and bottom right BethAnn Herman

p. 68: Debbie Moses Ketel

p. 71: Roxanne Horkey

p. 73: Verne's Photo Shop

p. 78: Jay Ketel

p. 79: Roger Flanagan

p. 85: Lincoln Borglum Collection

p. 91: Kim Taylor

p. 93: Kim Taylor

p. 99: Bell Photo

p. 102: Rodger Slott

p. 106: Chad Coppess

p. 118: South Dakota Tourism

p. 125: South Dakota Tourism

p. 128: Chad Coppess

p. 131: Ann Henrichsen

p. 132: Chad Coppess

p. 141: South Dakota Tourism

p. 152: Chad Coppess

p. 154: South Dakota Tourism

p. 158: NPS